The Shape of Baptism: The Rite of Christian Initiation

Studies in the Reformed Rites of the Catholic Church, Volume I

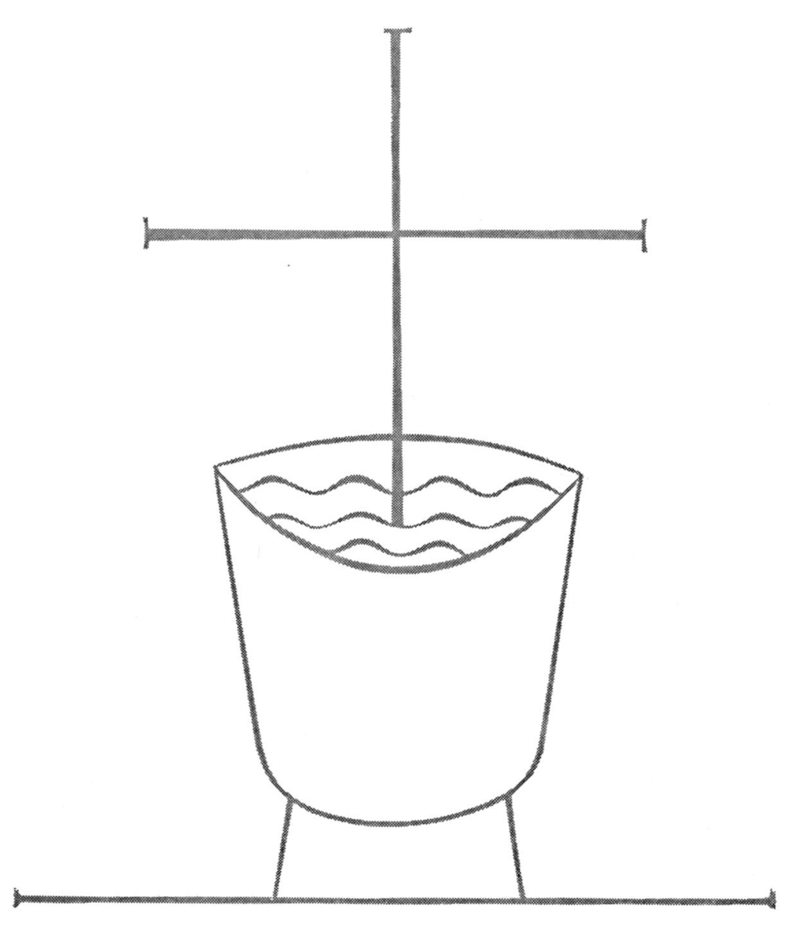

Aidan Kavanagh

The Shape of Baptism:
The Rite of Christian Initiation

A PUEBLO BOOK

The Liturgical Press Collegeville, Minnesota

Design: Frank Kacmarcik

Parts of Chapters 4 and 5 appeared originally in somewhat different form as "The Norm of Baptism: The New Rite of Christian Initiation of Adults," *Worship* 48 (1974) 143–152; "Christian Initiation of Adults: The Rites," *Worship* 48 (1974) 318–335; and in *Made, Not Born, New Perspectives on Christian Initiation and the Catechumenate,* ed. The Murphy Center for Liturgical Research (University of Notre Dame Press, Notre Dame, Indiana 1976) 118–137; and as "The New Roman Rites of Adult Initiation," *Studia Liturgica* 10:1 (1974) 35–47.

Scriptural pericopes quoted from the Revised Standard Version.

A Pueblo Book published by The Liturgical Press

Library of Congress Cataloging-in-Publication Data

Kavanagh, Aidan.
The shape of baptism : the rite of Christian initiation / Aidan Kavanagh.
p. cm.
"A Pueblo book."
Reprint. Originally published: New York : Pueblo Pub. Co., 1978.
Includes bibliographical references and index.
ISBN 0-8146-6036-3
1. Baptism. 2. Baptism (Liturgy) 3. Baptism—Catholic Church. 4. Catholic Church—Liturgy. I. Title.
BV800.K38 1991 91-12952
264'.02081—dc20 CIP

For
Kieran
Polycarp
and
Guy

Contents

Introduction

Two things prowl the thickets of the mind of one who would attempt a book meant to be of both theoretical and practical help to those concerned about Christian initiation.

The first is the hopelessness of doing justice to the literature on the subject. Spanning the better part of two thousand years, this literature simply cannot all be read, much less mastered by any one individual. Nor can its many seeming contradictions and equivocations, begotten in cultural differences and often sharpened by theological debate, be unraveled in a work of the scope and purpose represented in this one.

This being the case, the second thing is that a book on baptismal initiation need not attempt to settle all disputed questions or provide all the last words on biblical exegesis. It must not be a polemical tract or a mere tour through a ceremonial museum.

What seems needed, and what this book will try to be, is a practical analysis of a particular tradition of Christian initiation done from within that tradition but against the background of what was going on in other traditions as well. The particular tradition with which this book will be concerned is that of the Roman Rite. This tradition is a living thing, and analysis of it will have to be critical in both a positive and negative sense. It will also have to be discriminating, for as there remains a rich variety of initiatory practices in historic Christianity east and west, there also remains a real variety of initiatory practices within the communion of churches embraced by Catholicism itself.

History demonstrates that the Roman Church, while it has never abandoned or ceased to cherish catholicity, has never regarded itself as the only catholic church. Augustine's church was undoubtedly catholic: it was also Carthaginian rather than Roman, and a Latin church while its Roman sister had still been largely Greek-speaking. Catholic also were the northern Italian church of Ambrose of Milan, the Spanish church of Isidore and Ildephonse of Seville, and the Gallic churches of Hilary of Poitiers and Caesarius of Arles. These catholic churches celebrated non-Roman Latin liturgies which both presumed and fostered idioms of Christian thought and life that were themselves non-Roman. They affected many aspects of Roman Catholic tradition over the centuries, making it a river of breadth and depth rather than a pure if narrow stream. Nowhere is this fact more evident than in the evolution of initiatory practice in the specifically *Roman* Rite upon which this book will focus.

In attempting a practical analysis of Roman initiatory tradition, this book will be neither purely theoretical nor merely popular in its basic method. For a liturgical tradition is no more a theoretical abstraction than it is the popular enthusiasm of a given moment. The passage of time and much use discipline it into a sustained yet ever modulating *praxis*. As all living things do, a liturgical tradition embraces at every point both continuity and change, yet neither of these two characteristics is as vital as the tension that always exists between them. It is this vital tension that attracts analysis and often defies it, but it always requires an adequate methodology if even minimal results are to be obtained.

Every liturgy is traditional, and every tradition has a history. Yet scholars are often guilty of methodological ineptness when liturgical analysis is involved. They sometimes assume that a liturgy is a text. But a liturgy is not merely or even primarily a text. It is a complex of *acts* that have involved generations of people intellectually, emotionally, and sensually as well. To this complexity a liturgical text is merely the initial key. The information yielded by a liturgical text, where it has survived (and most have not), must be set among all the other data bearing on the original act—the spatial data of architecture, the visual data of the graphic and plastic arts, the sonic data of music and rhetoric, and all the rest—if one is to reach some degree of insight into what the act meant and means. Like a music critic, the student of liturgy must go beyond text if meaning is to be had. For liturgies are "composed" to be performed rather than read. Unlike composers of music, their authors are not individuals but whole peoples, and the composition evolves so slowly as a rule that the process is rarely remarked upon even by those who know it best.

Analyzing a liturgical "score" without benefit of much more than some fragments of a libretto is perilous, and its results are bound to be modest. Yet even this is something, especially if there remains oblique information on the way the performance went, and if its meaning and impact are still remembered and recounted among subsequent generations. One attempts analysis even under such adverse conditions only because not to do so leaves a certain amnesia in control of a generation's self-awareness—a condition that reduces its ability to function in the present and survive in the future. It is a risky business. But the risk is worth taking, and it will be taken here.

In doing this, a major point concerning method will be presumed without defense since this major point functions throughout the whole tradition under analysis. It is the presumption that because liturgical worship is the act of the Church, and that because the Church is before all else a community at prayerful worship before God in Christ, therefore worship precedes theological reflection and subordinates it. The classic Latin patristic position that the law of worship constitutes the law of belief, *legem credendi lex statuat supplicandi*,[1] is a formula of Prosper of Aquitaine (+ c. 465). This means more than that the liturgy as a whole is one source for theology among others. As Alexander Schmemann observes: "Liturgical tradition is not an 'authority' or a *locus theologicus*; it is the ontological condition of theology, of the proper understanding of *kerygma*, of the Word of God, because it is in the Church, of which the *leitourgia* is the expression and the life, that the sources of theology are functioning precisely as sources."[2]

This does not mean that every liturgical act is indiscriminately equal to all others, or that ceremonies are a substitute for faith. It does, however, mean that the liturgy as a whole is nothing other than the Church's faith in motion both at the highest and on the most practical levels. This faith surely has other modes and levels, but these are to be evaluated finally in terms of the Church at worship rather than vice versa. The liturgy does not merely reflect but actualizes concretely and in a sustained manner that basic repertoire of faith which is irreducible; it does this to a degree of regular comprehensiveness no other mode or level of faith-activity can equal. The liturgy is thus not merely one ecclesiastical "work" among many others. It is the Church living its life in which Christ is encountered regularly and dependably as in no other way.

Only this accounts for the fact that in historic Catholicism, liturgical modulation is most profoundly what gives rise to correlative doctrinal transpositions—as in the continuing evolution of theological reflection on the eucharist since the early medieval period in the west,[3] and the distillation of the classic creeds from the trinitarian questions put to catechumens at their baptism.[4] Nor did the practice of liturgical worship wait upon and depend from the written scriptures as a living illustration of the sacred texts. Rather, the written texts of the Christian bible, as they emerged, entered into worship patterns that were already established—especially in the synagogal, paschal, and domestic usages of Judaism which the earliest Christians continued to employ even as they began to fill them with a new content. The liturgy is scripture's home rather than its stepchild, and the Hebrew and Christian bibles were the Church's first liturgical books.[5]

Finally, it should soon occur to the reader that this book is about more than the act of baptism in water alone. For the liturgical sources all show that baptism involved more than this, and the New Testament at least implies it. The metaphor of washing has never exhausted all the teaching on baptism: it is but one feature in a much richer context of images.[6] The texts and ceremonies of the water bath therefore do not stand by themselves. They are part of a whole continuum of practices that will be referred to as "initiation" or as "baptism in its fullness" simply for lack of better generic terms to designate the whole ensemble of events associated with the making of a Christian. Nothing so subtly impedes obtaining an adequate grasp of water baptism itself, much less of Christian initiation as a whole, as the shrunken presumption that the event in water was all there ever was to it, and that all else constitutes highly problematic additions to this originally simple act, diluting it and rendering it opaque. Baptism has always been a compound act absorbing cultural patterns into itself: it has taken on definite shape in various cultures, shaping those cultures in turn.

The first two chapters following will therefore outline as concisely as possible how this repertoire of baptismal acts has been marshalled by salient Christian traditions into distinctive liturgical shapes. Emphasis will be laid in the second chapter on how conversion comes to be translated into communicable ecclesial modalities by catechesis in order to prepare both convert and Church for the Spirit-filled events of sacramental initiation, consecration, and rebirth.

The third, fourth, and fifth chapters will deal with the reforms of the Second Vatican Council touching initiatory practice in the Roman Rite—their context, basic thrust, and liturgical details as worked out by the various postconciliar commissions from the Council's end until 1972 when the *Ordo Initiationis Christianae Adultorum* was issued by the Holy See. The sixth chapter will comment on all this both theologically and pastorally, offering what will be more basic orientations for the future than detailed ceremonial recipes for all conceivable situations. A bibliography found at the end of the book contains works cited in text and notes. This is meant to be a helpful list for further reading, mainly in English, for those who wish to go further into some aspects treated in the book.

Thanks are due and sincerely tendered to Bernard Benziger and William Smith of Pueblo Publishing Company, old friends who prevailed upon me to write this volume and to edit a series of others under the general title "Studies in the Reformed Rites of the Catholic Church," based on the contents of their collection, *The Rites of the Catholic Church*; to Colin Williams, Dean of The Divinity School, Yale University, for arranging a semester's leave of absence that made it possible to finish the book; and to Sarai Schnucker and David Lancaster, who typed the manuscript.

Aidan Kavanagh, O.S.B
The Divinity School
Yale University
St. John the Baptist 1978

NOTES

1. See I. H. Dalmais, "La liturgie et le dépôt de la foi," in *L'Eglise en Prière*, ed. A. G. Martimort *et al*. (Desclée, Paris 1961) 220-228.

2. "Theology and Liturgical Tradition," in *Worship in Scripture and Tradition*, ed. Massey H. Shepherd (Oxford University Press, Oxford 1963) 175.

3. See the two works of J. A. Jungmann, *The Mass of the Roman Rite*, trans. F. X. Brunner (Benziger, New York 1950) 2 vols., and *The Place of Christ in Liturgical Prayer*, trans. A. Peeler (Alba House, Staten Island [2]1965).

4. See J. N. D. Kelly, *Early Christian Creeds* (Longmans, Green, London 1950).

5. See J. Daniélou, *The Bible and the Liturgy* (University of Notre Dame Press, Notre Dame, Indiana 1956).

6. Thus Charles Davis, *Sacraments of Initiation: Baptism and Confirmation* (Sheed and Ward, New York 1964) 9f.

The Tradition

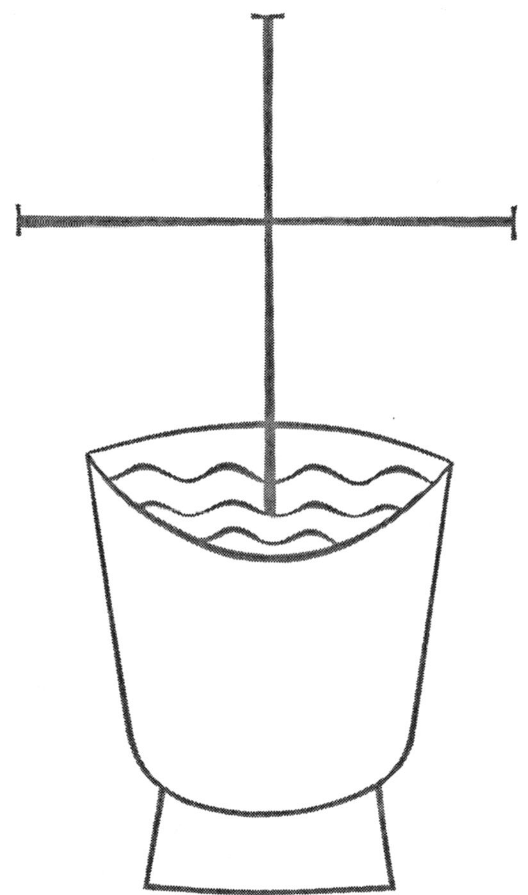

Chapter One

The Foundations

No New Testament text was, so far as we know, written prior to the paschal consummation of Jesus' life. All these texts, even those which purport to quote things said and describe things done prior to this, were written in the knowledge that the mystery had indeed begun to be lived by Jesus' followers in definite ways that were already becoming stable.

Yet evidence also suggests that the New Testament authors, like the incipient churches in which they lived and wrote, were obsessed with reporting accurately the facts of Jesus' life and ministry. And while their criteria for accuracy were broader than those with which a modern scholar would feel comfortable (chronology was for them less important than accurate interpretation of what had happened, and meaning more crucial than exact journalistic quotation), it remained central to their task to insist upon the historical veracity of the deeds they reported.

When, for example, the author of 1 John states that "This is he who came by water and blood, Jesus Christ, not with the water only but with the water and the blood" (5.6), he is in all probability engaging neither in a flight of mystical fancy nor in an attempt to provide a warrant of Christ's institution of the sacraments of baptism and eucharist for subsequent generations. He is much more likely refuting early gnostic opinions that held Jesus to have become the Christ only at his baptism, and to have ceased being the Christ as his passion began. It is the historical actuality of the incarnate life of Jesus Christ that is being asserted by the author of 1 John. "Jesus Christ," he says, "was baptized as flesh and blood and died as flesh and blood."[1]

But words of fact, while uttered with a specific object in mind, have a way of being received on more than one level, and this too forms the context of meaning within which human discourse takes place. Meaning is not only uttered. It is also perceived, and the two actions do not always wholly coincide. Truth, for New Testament authors at least, transcends exclusively factual accuracy. Thus, it is as probable as anything else that the *meaning-context* within which the author of 1 John asserts the historical actuality of the incarnate life of Jesus Christ picked up resonances in the words used, whether or not the author intended them, that transcended their use in an argument against gnostics. This *meaning-context* is postpaschal church life, within which such a document as the fourth gospel does not merely recount the events of Jesus' human life but, by a careful use of parabolic symbolism, depicts how that life has now overflowed its original boundaries to become communal and perennial: that is, ecclesial and eschatological.

In this instance of 1 John, as in the fourth gospel and so many other places in the New Testament, one must keep this methodological point in mind. The development of Christian patterns of life—including those of prayer, ethics, mysticism, and worship—did not wait upon the issuance of authoritative texts by New Testament authors to begin. These texts were written within such patterns and speak in their knowledge. They sometimes correct them, sometimes recommend them to others. They most frequently, however, presume them and pass over them in silence.

But that the patterns were there can be neither doubted nor discounted, even though their exact form cannot always be determined with scholarly precision.

A further example of this can be seen in 1 Corinthians 1.13-17, where Paul situates the taproot of christology in ecclesial and baptismal categories. Here he says that Christ is undivided and indivisible; that only he died for you and therefore you are his alone; thus were you baptized in his name and in that of no other. These affirmations are less mystical than they are rabbinical, juridicial, and ecclesial. Nor does v. 17, "For Christ did not send me to baptize but to preach the gospel. . . ," imply that Paul thought baptism unimportant. On the contrary, as Schnackenburg oberserves,

"In his churches all were baptized, and on this fact he built his teaching of the body of Christ (1 Cor. 12:13, Gal. 3:27f), which dominates his theology of the Church. He did not attempt to remove baptism to a distance from his theological construction, as if it were a foreign body, or to push it in a spare room, as it were; rather he was increasingly concerned to make it a corner stone of his Christ-related doctrine of salvation."[2]

Paul's theology of salvation reaches its high point in Romans 6.1-11 ("Do you not know that all of us who have been baptized into Christ Jesus were baptized into his death?"); his theology of the Church attains its summit in Ephesians 4.5 (". . . one Lord, one faith, one baptism . . ."). The power of the cross of Christ (1 Corinthians 1.17) erupts in the world through baptism celebrated continuously in the Spirit-filled Body of Christ which is the Church. Baptism is not an enacted metaphor based on the cross: baptism is the power of the cross made actual among those who believe. Baptism is thus the most immediate facet of the gospel that drives Paul to preach.

Yet in Paul, as in John and all the other New Testament authors, the references to baptism are more allusive than descriptive. Assuming the existence of baptismal patterns, these authors were concerned mainly to reflect on the patterns they knew, less to report how the patterns were carried out in detail. This fact does not, however, leave us wholly in the dark about the details of baptismal rites during the New Testament period. We do know, first, some specific details about the various ablutions, lustrations, and "baptisms" in Judaism, from which Christian practice undoubtedly grew. Second, the allusions of New Testament authors sometimes suggest details about the performance of the rite. Third, because the New Testament documents were not produced all at once but issued over a span of perhaps three generations after the death of Jesus, we can detect in them a growth of baptismal practice that takes us into the early years of the second century, when other witnesses such as the *Didache* (c. 100) and Justin Martyr (c. 150) become more detailed in describing initiatory structure as a whole.

ABLUTIONS AND BAPTISMS IN JUDAISM

The author of Hebrews 6.1-2 refers to instruction about "baptisms" other than that recognized as being of Christ as one of the well-known matters his hearers do not need to hear about again. These baptisms were already practiced prior to the resurrection and continued after it. As a genre of ritual acts they were multiform in Judaism.[3]

A holiness structure extends far back into the preliterary beginnings of Jewish religion. Like analogous structures,[4] it took concrete form in the ritual definitions of purity and impurity.[5] The structure as a whole was implacably objective:[6] impurity was contracted by contact with such numinous realities as blood, corpses or tombs, animals defined as "strange," or with persons suffering from certain diseases that were manifestly loathesome no matter what the subjectivity of the sullied person might be. Yet the focus of the matter rested not on the impure object but on the effect contact with it had upon the person, who was *ipso facto* rendered unfit for any relationship with God or, by extension, with his people. Ritual uncleanness thus resulted simultaneously in what we today would recognize as civil and religious excommunication.

Originally of an ontological rather than an ethical character, the nature and function of the impurity can be discerned in the rituals designed to avoid it (as in the rituals of food preparation and diet) or to overcome it. The latter in particular were largely rites involving water, sometimes specified as running water.[7] Their development was especially rapid in the New Testament era as the codification of earlier practices was undertaken by rabbinical schools.[8] Although the rites have nothing to do with forgiveness of sins, being applicable to things as well as persons, it is clear that they nonetheless contain implications for the ethical evolution of the holiness structure as well as images and elements which would be used by the prophets to internalize religious sentiment. For them, with the washing of bodies must go the cleansing of hearts.

In addition, however, to purification rituals, later Judaism knew a form of water rite which seems to have become more initiatory in character. This was the practice of proselyte baptism, and it seems to have developed in connection with the expansion of Jewish communities living outside Palestine.[9] By the second century of the Christian era, and probably earlier, the rite encompassed three phases: instruction concerning Israel's persecuted condition and the commandments of the Law, circumcision for males, and a water bath for all.[10] The central element in this ritual process, and demonstrably the oldest, was the act of male cirumcision by which solidarity with the holy nation of priests and kings (Exodus 19.6) was established in a most concrete way. But after the New Testament era rabbinical opinions began to differ over the role of the water bath and its relation to circumcision. Originally perhaps nothing more than the proselyte's first ritual purification after circumcision in preparation for the offering of sacrifice, the water bath begins later to absorb the initiatory aspects of circumcision, finally to displace circumcision in some places altogether as the central act by which a gentile adhered to Judaism. This development would have been spurred by the enactment of civil laws against circumcision in some areas, by a pastoral desire to accommodate gentiles as the active solicitation of converts increased in the early years of the Christian era, and as what would be called the "baptist movement" sprang up on the edges of official Judaism.[11]

If this is true, then by the Christian era proselyte *baptism* would have been assuming an increasingly initiatory character despite its fundamentally purificatory history and nature. The divergence of rabbinical opinions on the ritual necessity of circumcision and the nature of the water bath seems to support this hypothesis, indicating that in the early years of the Christian era older ritual forms were being invested with altered meaning in response to pastoral needs. The purificatory form of the water bath for proselytes remained while taking on at least some of the initiatory meaning traditionally associated with circumcision. The bath existed, with or without circumcision, to make gentiles Jews. It did this by purifying converts *from* their uncleanness and by admitting them *into* the covenant life of Judaism which was consummated by the offering of sacrifice.

The actual rite of proselyte baptism illustrates basic ablutionary procedure in later Judaism. It involved a full bath (*tebilah*) in considerable amounts of water, not just a minimal sprinkling with a few drops. The kind of water to be used depended, of course, upon what was available in a semiarid climate, but for ritual purposes water was ranked in six degrees in ascending order of value: 1) puddled water, 2) caught rain water, 3) water in a container holding forty "seals," 4) water from a fountain, 5) salty water or hot spring water, 6) "living" water, i.e., cold running water in a natural conduit such as a stream or river.[12] Because the water had to come into immediate contact with all parts of the body, nakedness was required and accoutrements such as cosmetics, jewelry, ribbons, clothing, or hygenic devices had to be removed.[13] Thus immersion seems to be implied as well.[14] A specification for the washing of proselytes was that the commandments of Torah, which had served as the foundation of their preliminary instruction, were recited to the proselyte as he or she stood in the water, for it was into these commandments as a way of living that one would be baptized.

In addition, the whole process by which a gentile could become a Jew gave rise to a body of teaching about conversion that stressed the radicalness of the move. "The view that conversion from heathenism to Judaism implies a new life, whether a dying and a rising again, or a new birth, is firmly attested in the Talmud."[15] Rabbinical epigrams such as "One who separates himself from his uncircumcision is like one who separates himself from the grave," and "One who has beccme a proselyte is like one newly born," give the flavor of this teaching and enhance the degree of probability that New Testament baptismal catecheses (e.g., John 3 and Romans 6) were greatly influenced by it.

But the opinion of some scholars that Christian baptism itself was genetically derived from proselyte baptism is unlikely.[16] On the matter of practice, New Testament evidence linking Christian baptism to proselyte baptism is not only lacking, but what evidence there is points instead toward Jesus' own baptism by John the Baptist in the Jordan as the prototype of Christian practice. In the scriptural accounts of the Baptist's teaching there is no hint of a death–resurrection theme, no initiatory motif, and no trace of proselyte baptism's admission of a convert to the sacrificial cult of Israel. John's emphases dwell rather upon prophetic expectations of the divine cleansing to be consummated by the work of the promised Messiah in a time of greatly heightened eschatological hope. John's baptism of repentance is preparatory for the messianic work. It is not a means for making gentiles Jews, as was proselyte baptism, nor is it wholly bounded by the bathing ablutions of the Essene ascetics or Qumran.[17] It is its own distinctive thing, subsequently viewed by New Testament authors as the opening of a new order of things without actually being included in it.[18] John's baptism is in water: it will give way to another baptism by One who will baptize with Holy Spirit and with a judgment finer than fire.[19] So immediate is this expectation that John himself regarded his baptism as a temporary rite which brought the prophets' insistence on moral renewal and official Judaism's emphasis on ritual purity together into a final synthesis shot through with messianic hope.[20] The Messiah's appearance on the scene will transform this synthesis into something quite new. All four gospels stress that

Jesus submitted himself to John's baptism both as to its content and its form. Its content was based on costly preaching and witness; it demanded conversion of life as precondition as well as its continuing outcome; it promised remission of sins. In submitting to its ritual form, Jesus established his solidarity with those who were the objects of John's preaching. Yet John's baptism became the prototype of Christian procedure not because of some quality inherent in it, but because of what happened when it was applied to Jesus—a happening that at once consummated John's baptism and rendered it obsolete. In John's baptism of Jesus the Old Covenant did not so much come to an end as mutate into the New by the agency of a divine act manifesting Jesus as the Messiah of God.

THE NEW TESTAMENT

From the foregoing it is clear that in the time of the New Testament several attitudes concerning ritual purification in water were already in place within the religious milieu. First, there existed a body of teaching centered on proselyte baptism that was not only concerned with objective ritual purity but also with the interior ethical and initiatory aspects that were involved in the whole conversion process. Circumcision still played a crucial role in this process, but some rabbinical schools began to emphasize the water bath increasingly. Second, while the Christian prototype of baptism is that of Jesus' baptism by John in the Jordan rather than proselyte baptism as such, nonetheless *the body of teaching* centering on proselyte baptism would have provided a significantly rich repertoire of images and procedures for the earliest Christian baptismal catecheses. Third, the analogies that developed between Jewish and Christian practice were not so at variance that even in polemical exchanges the same term could not be used by the early fathers to compare Jewish baths and Christian baptism.[21] Fourth, there are no grounds for thinking that Christians turned a purely mechanical Jewish ablution ritual into a deeply interiorized moral event—a dead "work" into a symptom of lively "faith," or a priestly religion into a prophetic one. To anachronize in this manner is to assume that prophet and priest, or heart and cult, were opposed options in Judaism. The ritual development of proselyte baptism, as well as the evolution of ascetical ablutionary practices and the emergence of John's baptism out of both of them in a period of intense messianic expectation, belie this view. Indeed, even these have to be seen against the backdrop of later Judaism's increasing sophistication regarding the moral and purificatory expectations even the temple cult demanded, as Psalms 24 and 51 witness.[22] Fifth, as there was no doubt in later Judaism about whether a gentile could become a Jew, so there was no doubt in early Christianity about whether a gentile could become a Christian. In both cases, discussion centered not upon whether but upon how this was to be done. The question being common, answers in practice can be expected to be similar if not identical.

With these things in mind, it is necessary to note that the New Testament does not use the term "baptism" univocally. Not only did New Testament authors know "baptisms" that were not Christian (Hebrews 6.1-2); they also knew three sets of baptismal practices that pertained specifically to Christian usage far more than did Jewish or pagan ablutions.

Jesus' Baptism by John

The first of these was the baptism of Jesus by John in the Jordan. This was not the same as John's other baptisms, for in this particular baptism something unique and wholly without precedent occurred. One of the many who came to receive a conversion baptism for the remission of sins was perceived by John to be, and then was divinely manifested as, both the King-Messiah and the Servant of the Lord foretold by the prophets (Matthew 3.13-17). Both prophetic images were richly complex, and their being focused in Jesus produced the earliest strata of understanding about who he was and what he came to do. He is the Warrior Lamb (Apocalypse 6.16, 17.14) who will triumph and judge vigorously (Matthew 3.11-12). But he is also the Lamb slain for the world's sins (Apocalypse 5.6–12.11), the paschal sacrifice (John 19.37, Isaiah 53.7). John 1.29-30 draws both these strands together to enunciate a doctrine of Jesus the Christ as preexistent Messiah who comes to his baptism and his task in solidarity with his people rather than in substitution for them. Lord of all yet first-born of his people, he can uniquely represent them to God and mediate God to them. In his baptism, Jesus joins the ranks of the Faithful Remnant, creates it the cornerstone of a new world, and embarks upon the eschatological task assigned the Messiah of God.

In this view, Jesus' own baptism is both in contact with John's baptism and yet at some distance from it.[23] Similarly, Jesus' own baptism is undoubtedly the source of Christian baptism yet different from it as well. What New Testament writers stress is the uniqueness of Jesus' baptism rather than its resemblances to later sacramental practice. Christian baptism is seen by them not as an attempt to mimic Jesus' baptism in the Jordan but as the primary if still developing event by which the Church responds to and appropriates under grace the "total redemptive action which the baptism of Jesus set in motion."[24] Christian practice is based not on isolated moments: it is a coherent history that knows not only John's adumbration of redemption and its beginning with Jesus' baptism. It also knows its accomplishment in the resurrection (Matthew 28.18) and its consummation in the parousia. It is into this *whole* sweep of redemptive activity that Christian initiation splices one.[25]

Prepaschal Baptisms

The second set of baptismal practices mentioned in the New Testament is that of the period after Jesus' baptism by John but before the resurrection. There is no report in the synoptic gospels that Jesus himself baptized at all during his ministry. The fourth gospel says at one point that Jesus did baptize; at another that he did not baptize but authorized his disciples to do so (John 3.22f; 4.1-4). Although faced with silence on one hand and a seeming contradiction on the other, one need not conclude that the matter of baptisms during Jesus' ministry is a dilemma at worst or paradox at best. The gospels' evidence is not so impenetrable, even though it is admittedly not as detailed as one might wish. The gospels do tell us clearly that baptism continued to be practiced in Jesus' circle; that Jesus' baptisms (whether performed by him or by his growing number of disciples at his behest) undoubtedly began to take on a messianic emphasis that conformed more to his own ministry as distinct from that of John's, thus creating a certain tension between the two men's followers; that an overweening concern with water baptism seems to fade in the consciousness of Jesus and his circle as his ministry moves away from the wilderness and into the cities, bearing its messianic message. As this movement increases in speed and intensity, the "baptism with which I must be baptized" (Mark 10.38, Luke 12.50) seems to grow in Jesus' consciousness. "He is to be plunged, not into water but into calamity unto death."[26] Subsequent tradition (e.g., Romans 6) will look back to this event and its results rather than to John's baptisms or to Jesus' own baptism at his hands as the proximate foundation for Christian baptismal teaching and practice.

In this perspective, the prepaschal baptisms of Jesus' ministry were therefore no longer Jewish or johannine, nor were they yet "Christian": they were baptism "in obedience to the messianic proclamation, under the sign of the messianic action and in anticipation of the messianic deliverance."[27] Beyond this one can only observe that, whatever else they may have been, New Testament writers apparently do not regard them as exhibiting a pneumatic nature appropriate to a Messiah who will come baptizing not with water but with Holy Spirit (John 1.33). None of the sources report pneumatic occurrences connected with any baptisms prior to the resurrection, the first such account being that of the outpouring of the Spirit upon the gathering at Pentecost— a pure pneumatic baptism without use of water. The experience impells Peter to the first recorded proclamation which speaks not of the pouring out of water but of the Spirit upon all flesh as the true baptism to which all must come by repentance and a conversion bath for the forgiveness of sins (Acts 2).

The unavoidable implication in this is that Peter's hearers must come to the fullness of messianic redemption in Christ's poured-out Spirit by the same route Peter and his colleagues had come, namely, by repentance and a post-johannine water bath authorized by Jesus the Messiah—a water bath thus differentiated from all others by its relationship to the Messiah so as to be "in his name." The prepaschal baptisms performed during Jesus' ministry are by this not so much rendered obsolete as they are transmuted and raised to a level of actualized completion by the pentecostal event. Jesus' baptism with Holy Spirit, which John prepared for and predicted, is now revealed through the agency of his own death and resurrection to be both cause and effect of water baptism. The two baptisms merge without confusion to become the moment of the Church's birth, the condition of its life, and the content of its mission (Matthew 28.18f).[28]

Postpaschal Baptisms

In the Pentecost account (Acts 2.1-39), the immediate result of the outpouring of the Spirit upon the closed gathering is Peter's proclamation of its having happened, and of all that led up to it, to the multitude of "Jews and devout men from every nation under heaven" assembled in Jerusalem for the feast. His speech to them ends in a call to be *baptized in repentance*, "in the name of Jesus Christ for the forgiveness of your sins," and with a promise that they will receive the "gift of the Holy Spirit." The context does not demand that one find here a description of liturgical sequence, perhaps forced on the original chaotic event by later editors who knew a settled liturgical order in which preaching, baptism, and the gift of the Spirit are sequentially ordered. More likely, the assembled multitude is being called upon to turn from "this crooked generation" (Acts 2.40) by entering the company of those who have witnessed with their own eyes the exaltation of the anointed Holy One of God through the same process they themselves had undergone, namely, through a conversion baptism for the forgiveness of sins in the name of no one other than the *Christos-Messiah* himself, who baptizes with Spirit. The initiatory pattern in Acts 2 probably is not that of a later church but of the pentecostal community itself. The Spirit begins to be lived in water baptism: it is not received as an added gift after, as a cake receives its frosting. Concerning the some three thousand who responded to Peter's call that day, Acts notes that they were baptized, "And they devoted themselves to the apostles' teaching and fellowship, to the breaking of bread and the prayers" (2.42). That is, they began to live the Spirit-life of the faithful community. This living communally in the Spirit seems to be given priority over the charismatic manifestations that such living results in, including the "signs and wonders" that continued to be done through the apostles resident in the Jerusalem church (2.43-47).

There can be little doubt that the stunning experience of "Spirit baptism" on the first Pentecost, with its ensuing conversions and the establishment of the premier church in Jerusalem, exercised a profound influence both on the earliest churches' understanding of Jesus' own baptism and on subsequent initiatory practice. The revelations of the Pentecost occurrence cannot but have influenced the ways in which the evangelists later would interpret Jesus' baptism by John in their very accounts of it. In these, as we have seen, great stress is put upon its contrast to the baptisms John regularly performed. This stress is marked by the deeply symbolic and therefore meaning-laden use of spirit imagery, and it probably was given finer point by the increasing use of ritual acts of anointing, present in the culture, as its pivotal referent.

While the synoptic gospels make no explicit reference to Jesus' being "anointed" in the Jordan, Acts 10.38 does refer to him as the One whom God "anointed with Holy Spirit and with power." And in Luke 4.18 Jesus applies Isaiah 61.1-2 to himself: "The Spirit of the Lord has been given to me, for he has anointed me." These references suggest that the postpentecostal church had begun to understand the dovelike descent of the Spirit and the voice's saying "You are my beloved Son, my favor rests upon you" (Luke 3.22) as constituting Jesus' anointment and investment as *Christos-Messiah*, the anointed King of prophecy.[29]

This event, rather than the descent into the waters of the Jordan, is what the synoptics emphasize. Looking back after Pentecost, "It is clear . . . that when the evangelists tell us about this baptism they are thinking of the baptism of Christians: the visible manifestation of the Spirit foreshadows baptism in the Spirit, and the Father's designation of the Son points towards the adoption of the baptized as sons . . . Christian living constantly made Jesus' followers think back to the mysterious act which lay at the foundation of their new condition."[30]

When the evangelists wrote, baptism was a crucial set of acts already beginning to undergo ritualization and stabilization in the churches. Its Spirit-emphasis, together with the symbolic and ritual "vocabulary" of anointing, are salient facts that must therefore be kept to the forefront in analyzing the earliest growth of baptismal practice. Due to the relative simplicity of the water ablution and to its being both widespread and well known even prior to the Christian era, it comes into use in the earliest churches with relatively few ritual elaborations being necessary—except in a growing specification of the number of immersions and of the precise words to be said in connection with them. More ritually significant will be the evolution of ways in which to manifest the pneumatic nature of this ablutionary event both by proclamation and by acts.

If the foregoing is true, it helps to account for the need felt after Pentecost to complete the baptisms whether of John, of Jesus' earlier disciples,[31] of gentiles who have believed and received the Spirit but have not been baptized in water,[32] or of Samaritans who have received baptism but not the Spirit's gifts.[33] The completion always consists in proclaiming the paschal-pentecostal Good News so that the hearers might "believe."[34] This usually resulted in baptism, but sometimes the Spirit was received immediately as a consequence of the apostolic proclamation, with baptism following.[35] These latter instances (to call them exceptions would be to anachronize), when taken together with the completion by Peter and John of Philip's baptism of the Samaritans, seem to suggest that the water bath had always to be situated in a context of having heard and believed in the Good News of the Lord's exaltation, together with some manifest relationship to the apostolic and pentecostal mother church of Jerusalem. The apostolic ministry provided this context for the water bath by preaching the Good News as eyewitnesses and by manifesting the relationship to the Jerusalem community through the fellowship gesture of laying hands on the newly baptized. Thus the manifestations of the Spirit may be seen as tied less to a *single act* in the process than as the result of complete absorption into communion with those of apostolic and paschal-pentecostal faith—a community in which the Spirit of the Anointed One is abroad, working its wonders as it will.

This in turn may help to account for the way water baptism and the perceptible outpouring of the Holy Spirit seem to be connected in New Testament reports—not so much in a rigid chronological sequence as in a tandem-like relationship whose common center of gravity is the risen and exalted *Christos-Messiah*. Both water baptism and the outpouring of the Spirit are necessary, but it is of less importance to note which comes first than to realize how *both* follow upon the proclamation of Jesus' resurrection and exaltation. All three of these events—proclamation, baptism, and the outpouring of Spirit—constitute the integrity of initiation into the believing community, the locale of the Spirit which is the Church. What one is confronted with in the New

Testament is not a set of separate and sometimes competing initiatory events but an initiatory continuum in the earliest stages of evolution.

The events, whose common ground is faith-life in the exalted Lord, begin to reveal a discernible degree of articulation with each other as that faith-life continues to take on ecclesial form. While this baptismal faith and practice takes its origin from above, owing its inception not to prophet or culture or John the Baptist or practices of the Law (being more in contrast to all these than congruous with them), it is nonetheless *one* (Ephesians 4.4-6, Hebrews 6.2) and already has begun to marshal into itself specific practices taken from Jewish and gentile patterns of life known to the community.

These specific practices, richly multivalent in their original contexts, take on new weights of meaning as they enter the initiatory continuum of baptismal faith and practice. Former meanings become redirected as they focus on this faith in practice, and in the process their multivalency mutates without being destroyed. The principles by which this welter of meanings can be classified to some degree are, however, to be found not only in the specific practices themselves (e.g., anointing and hand-laying) but more fundamentally in the basic initiatory structure that gives them shape even as they begin to inhabit it. To interpret the meaning of specific baptismal practices one must therefore pay attention to the whole initiatory structure that underlies and catalyzes them. In the New Testament period this basic initiatory structure consists of the following.

First in both sequence and importance, *the proclamation of the gospel* (at the highest degree of its integrity by an apostolic eyewitness of the life, death, resurrection, and exaltation of the Lord) *always precedes bap-*

tism. The only exception to this is Paul, who receives not a mediated proclamation of the gospel but a direct revelation of the Exalted One himself (Acts 9.1-19). This event constitutes Paul an eyewitness and is the basis of his claim to be an apostle. Yet he must nonetheless undergo water baptism at the hands of Ananias. The reason for this may well be that, despite the extraordinary personal revelation he had received, Paul had not previously received either the baptism of John or any prepaschal baptism at the hands of Jesus' followers: he stood in no relation to any of those who had undergone a baptism of repentance for the forgiveness of sins—a relationship which, as we have seen, seems to have been presumed in the pentecostal church of Jerusalem.[36]

Second, the normal response of those who hear the gospel proclaimed is expected to be conversion to faith in the exalted Lord. This conversion is sometimes of such a quality as to be accompanied by an overt outpouring of the Spirit even prior to baptism, especially if the hearers already stand in some prepaschal baptist tradition and receive the gospel from an apostolic eyewitness who can link the hearers in himself to the pentecostal Jerusalem community. When these conditions are lacking, even apostolic preaching preceding conversion, and baptism following it, do not suffice to elicit the outpouring of the Spirit.[37]

Third, the gospel proclaimed and believed usually results in the water bath itself. Sometimes an outpouring follows the proclamation, as we have seen, often in connection with hands being laid on the newly baptized by an apostle. This fact is in no way a denigration of water baptism, nor does it suggest that water baptism and "Spirit baptism" were competing liturgical forms in the earliest Christian communities.[38] Rather, the fact underlines the fundamentally pneumatic character of all postpaschal baptismal practice as distinct from the numerous other *baptismoi* of both Judaism and paganism at the time. It seems that Acts 10.44-48 and 11.15-16 should be read against this background.

A formula of words to be said in the baptismal act itself is usually either not reported or did not exist. There seems little reason to doubt that, after a lengthy and vigorous apostolic proclamation of the gospel, sometimes concluding with an overt outpouring of the Spirit, the act of immersion in water either in the apostle's witnessing presence or at his very hands spoke for itself. Thus when one reads of baptism in the name of Jesus or in the name of Father, Son, and Holy Spirit (e.g., Matthew 28.20), these phrases are probably less liturgical formulae than they are theological declarations in a judaic idiom on the binding nature of one's adherence to Christ in baptism.[39]

Fourth, there are *the events that follow water baptism*. The clearest recorded list of these is in Acts 2.42: "And they devoted themselves [after baptism] to the apostles' teaching (*didache*) and fellowship (*koinonia*), to the breaking of bread (*klasei tou artou*) and prayers (*proseuchais*)." In other words, what apostolic proclamation, conversion, and baptism in water and Spirit—the whole initiatory process— resulted in was life in a Spirit-filled community living by apostolic teaching, in unity with apostolic witness of the risen Lord who is exalted and now become life-giving Spirit for his people, through eucharistic prayer at home and petitionary prayer in the synagogue. The regular postbaptismal events at this period are not a series of specific liturgical "completions" of an only partial water rite, but full and robust engagement in the Church itself: a whole new ethic and way of life.

In sum, one may conclude that the rationale knitting together Christianity's earliest initiatory structure is something like this. *Preceded by authentic proclamation of the risen and exalted* Christos-Messiah *and by conversion, Spirit baptism by water at apostolic hands initiates one into the full life of the community in which the gospel has begun to become praxis*. Here is the common ground that serves as articulation point for all the multivalent practices that enter the initiatory continuum.

BAPTISM IN NEW TESTAMENT CHURCHES

In the three-generation span of New Testament literature there are allusions to the fact that the process of ritualizing Christian initiation in all its aspects had not only begun but reached considerable levels of development. This should be less surprising than that the process should not have taken place at all. Conversion to the *Christos-Messiah* undoubtedly produced a society of persons that was in marked contrast to all others, but neither the New Testament nor the apostolic tradition to which its era gave rise offer any sustained evidence that such a conversion deculturalized the convert or desocialized the Church. Despite certain deracinating effects which adherence to the *Christos-Messiah* certainly produced, there is no reason to think that the earliest Christian communities thereupon forsook their Jewishness or even their continued attendance at Jewish worship events (e.g., Acts 3.1; 17.10). Indeed, a towering problem for apostolic churches from the beginning was whether they could accept the risks of being transposed into a gentile key. Nor was the obverse of this problem absent either, namely, whether the churches could afford to remain within Judaism given the mounting hostility that was early in evidence, exemplified by the stoning of Stephen and the pogrom led by Saul (Acts 7.54–8.3).

It cannot escape notice that every surviving piece of New Testament literature seems to have been composed originally in Greek, although Hebraic phraseology and thought patterns regularly show through. An evolution is thus already evident in the language of the New Testament period itself, for language involves not only words but a whole culture as well. That the transposition of a new religious idiom from the culture of its origin into another one takes place exclusively on the level of words is not possible. For transposition in language necessitates cultural shift; cultural shift involves social change; and social change makes ritual modulation inevitable. Furthermore, no more radical events can affect societies than shifts in their language and ritual, and these shifts are invariably correlative. Peter and Paul confronted each other over this; it separated Christianity and Judaism in some rancor; and it also probably spelt the ultimate demise of the Jerusalem church's influence after 46 A.D., when the decision was taken to allow gentile forms of Christianity to evolve without hindrance from the Law (Acts 15.1-29).

It seems necessary to say all this here lest evidence touching the further ritualization of Christian initiation in the New Testament be obscured. As we have seen, a continuum of initiatory practice is not only in place there, it is also in evolution. The suggestion met with in some exegetical works by modern authors that the ritualization process began only later—reaching a sort of frenzy by the fourth century and marking a departure from New Testament purity of doctrine and practice—is polemical, anachronistic, and largely without merit. No evidence exists to show that the churches of the New Testament regarded themselves as a single incandescent experience of conversion manifested by occasional outbursts of glossolalia, and remembered by bible study groups that claimed to have some special insight into the hidden meaning of the Word granted to no one else.

Indeed, whenever this attitude raised its head it was quickly cautioned against by the apostolic tradition from Paul to Clement, to Irenaeus and beyond, as unauthentic and sectarian.

There is more unanimity in tradition and among modern scholars on the firm place proclamation of the gospel, conversion, and the water bath have in New Testament initiatory practice, however, than there is on the matter of the outpouring of the Spirit and its progressive ritualization both in the New Testament period and after. Yet there can be little doubt that the New Testament period viewed proclamation and conversion as the first two stages in one Spirit-laden process which was regularly consummated by a water bath that was itself the anointing and sealing of one's adherence to Christ in the same Spirit (e.g., 2 Corinthians 1.21-22). Life in the Spirit, poured out through the baptism of the Anointed One heralded by John, was so crucial that it had to be ritually manifested in more than one instance and in more than one way. Thus the growing standardization of the ways in which the gospel was proclaimed can be regarded as one type of ritualizing the pouring out of the Spirit in the initiation process. This standardization can be studied in Peter's pentecostal proclamation in Acts 2.14-36, in Stephen's in Acts 7.2-53, in the brief report of Philip's words to the eunuch in Acts 8.27-35, in the many proclamations that form the core of Paul's letters, and on into the first six chapters of the *Didache* on the way of teaching prior to baptism.

It must be remembered that the baptism of Christians was not johannine but christic: it was a baptism not of water but of Holy Spirit. The water bath is a function of the Spirit. This means that pneumatic data concerning Christian baptism subordinate water data: the latter are to be understood in terms of the former.

This alters the usual approach adopted by scholars looking for evidence of initiatory ritualization in the New Testament. It amounts to suggesting that one should give less consideration to the exclusive primacy of the water bath as something to which Spirit-related events are added much later as secondary elements. The crucial centrality of the Spirit of the Anointed One in New Testament reflection on the nature of faith makes it extremely unlikely that the Spirit's role in the whole process by which one entered the faith community could have been left unritualized altogether, or was allowed to be expressed only in the ritual of a johannine-appearing water bath. This should alert one to the probability that when New Testament texts refer, especially in passing, to "baptism" they mean something ritually larger and increasingly more sophisticated and complex than the water bath alone.

If this is *not* presumed, then it becomes impossible to account for how rites particularly related to the Spirit and in closer ritual contact with the water bath than proclamation prior to it, *suddenly* appear as though from nowhere during the second and third centuries. Nor does it explain why these rites quickly become accepted as traditional in churches obsessed with fidelity to the gospel and apostolic tradition.

If this *is* presumed, then two notable things are thrown into higher relief. The first is that one should give more ritual weight to direct, indirect, and even implied references to anointing in the New Testament itself. Given its insistence on the messianic "unction" of Jesus by the Spirit, and on his baptism being with Spirit rather than water, there seems to be at least as much reason to expect that actual anointings would concretize this for Jesus' followers, especially after Pentecost, as would a ritual ablution in water. The *exclusive* use of water to bring home to those adhering to the *Christos-Messiah* that they have become *christoi*, a People of "anointed" priests and kings in his Spirit, may be a later prejudice more than a contemporary New Testament fact. The water bath alone could, moreover, recommend to Christians precisely what the four gospels are at pains to deny, namely, that John's baptism in water rather than Jesus' baptism with Spirit was to be the norm for Christian attitude and practice. Apart from special charismatic manifestations of the Spirit's involvement throughout the initiatory process of proclamation, conversion, and water baptism (manifestations which were not inevitable and seem in Paul's letter to be a growing area for counterfeit charisms and a source of divisions), there could have been no more forceful way to stabilize the messianic and pneumatic character of all adherence to Christ than by actually anointing the baptized.

Anointing had as recognized a place, if not an even more exalted one, in the Jewish repertoire of religious acts as water ablution. In view of this, why the earliest churches should have been driven to ritual literalism concerning water but not concerning unction is a question that produces more ingenuities among modern authors than convincing answers. For example, the text of 1 John 2.20, "You have an anointing (*chrisma*) from the Holy One and you know all things," together with that of 2 Corinthians 1.21, "It is God who establishes us with you in Christ (*christon*) and has anointed us (*chrisas*)," lead most authors to think that here one may find the sort of attitude that *later* gave rise to actual anointings.[40] It is probable that in their literary contexts these two sayings use "anointing" figuratively. In Paul's case "anointing" is one figure used along with those of "sealing" and "earnest money," all of which refer to a Christian's reception of the Spirit without their being each assigned to specific ritual acts. In John's case it seems that *chrisma* is a figure for the truth of the gospel which causes the faithful community to know all things.

Granting this, however, one must question not only whether it took communities prepared to be ritually literal about washing metaphors up to a century and a half to become similarly disposed regarding unction, but also whether, when they finally did so, they had to steal the practice from gnosticism.[41] Furthermore, in the texts cited above the robustness of the anointing metaphor is enhanced rather than weakened if the process of Christian initiatory reception of the Spirit at the time was coming to know actual anointing as part of it.

A second thing the New Testament's emphasis on the pneumatic nature of baptism throws into higher relief is that the bath metaphor encompassed at the time a larger and more complex reality than the act of washing alone. Particularly in the antique Mediterranean world, bathing meant more than washing away dirt. One washed clothes or dishes, but one bathed oneself. The bath was a personal and, often, a social ritual the significance of which the modern world is perhaps only beginning to recover. One thus anachronizes when one imputes to someone like Paul, in whose writings the image of bathing occurs repeatedly, a later perception of the act as going no further than a quick shower mainly for purposes of personal hygiene.

This is not the place for an essay on the cultural and psychological significance of the bath. One can only note that more was involved in the bathing process then, and hence more was implied in the bathing metaphor when used by antique authors, than is the case today. While one obviously could wash without bathing as one could eat without dining, both acts took on vastly enriched social and personal importance as they were ritualized, becoming freighted with more than merely utilitarian meaning in the process. The surviving Roman baths found throughout the Mediterranean area, Europe, and the Middle East testify to this. The New Testament corpus brings both this social pattern and the religious washing and bathing patterns found in Judaism to bear as it seeks to express what adherence to Christ in the Spirit means for Christian faith and practice. Receiving the Spirit through Christ is likened to a *birth bath* in John 3.3-5 and Titus 3.5-7; to a *funeral bath* and burial in Romans 6.1-11; to a bride's *nuptial bath* in Ephesians 5.26. These cultural practices were consummated in anointing and in arraying the body in clean, new, or otherwise special clothing (Galatians 3.27) as the final stages of the bath itself.[42]

Especially in Paul's letters, this rich cultural usage and the usual human responses to it are orchestrated to convey on both conscious and preconscious levels something of what entry into communion with Christ in his Church involves. While New Testament authors should not be thought of as being concerned to report directly on ceremonial in current use, much less to draw up new ceremonies for the future, they did presume current usage, both sacred and secular, and invoked many of its aspects in their own theological reflection and authoritative instruction to the churches. Paul's own reflection upon and instruction about adherence to Christ, as a case in point, provide special testimony to the undiminished vigor of bath-usage that existed in the churches to which he wrote. *Soteriologically*, this adherence is a washing away of sin (1 Corinthians 6.11). The Church has been through this bath like a bride—refreshing, renewing, adorning, and fundamentally regenerating itself in all its members. *Christologically*, the bath plunges one into the "name of Jesus" (1 Corinthians 1.13, Acts 19.5) so profoundly that it sets Christians apart from all else as circumcision did the Jews (Colossians 2.11), arraying them in him (Galatians 3.27) and burying them in him (Romans 6.1-11, Colossians 3.11f) so totally that they become participants in his own ascent to his Father as Israel participated in Moses' passage from Egypt through the waters of the Red Sea and ultimately to the Promised Land (1 Corinthians 10.1-5). *Ecclesiologically*, the bath initiates the cleansed ones into a new People, the Body of Christ, the locale of his life-giving Spirit (1 Corinthians 12.13, 27). This results in their living in a community so new and different that conventional social analogues can hardly be used to describe it (Galatians 3.28, 1 Corinthians 13.12, Colossians 3.11).[43] So radically incomparable is this transformation in Christ-become-life-giving-Spirit that only the most primal human experiences such as marriage, birth, death, and dining together offer clues to it.

To these clues must finally be added the primal human need and experience of worship. Already in the New Testament, and after it in the earliest churches, one finds repeatedly the typological stress on Christian baptism as the initiation of those who, now purified of all uncleanness, are to approach God in worship. Arising from deep within Judaism (e.g., Exodus 19.6), this stress undergirds the whole continuum of its ablutionary practice and flows intensified into Christianity (e.g., Ephesians 2.11-22, Hebrews 10.19-39, 1 Peter 1.22–2.10, Apocalypse 1.5f).[44] As Nils Dahl observes: "In the baptismal liturgy and theology of the Ancient Church sacerdotal ideas are especially connected with post-baptismal anointing. But the whole, complex ceremony of Christian initiation, including water-baptism, change of clothes, anointing and first communion corresponds to the pattern of the Old Testament initiation of priests—much closer than to the rites for Jewish proselytes."[45]

And through all these clues, knitting them together, runs the fugal theme of the bath in its fullness.[46]

NOTES

1. G. R. Beasley-Murray, *Baptism in the New Testament* (Macmillan, New York 1962) 237.

2. R. Schnackenburg, *Baptism in the Thought of St. Paul*, trans. G. R. Beasley-Murray (Blackwell, Oxford 1964) 20-21.

3. See J. Delorme, "The Practice of Baptism in Judaism at the Beginning of the Christian Era," in *Baptism in the New Testament. A Symposium*, trans. D. Askew (Geoffrey Chapman, London 1964) 25-60; Beasley-Murray 1-44; Schnackenburg 8-9.

4. See, for example, Mary Douglas, *Purity and Danger: An Analysis of Concepts of Pollution and Taboo* (Routledge and Kegan Paul, London 1966).

5. See Leviticus 17–26.

6. On impersonal rules see Mary Douglas, *Natural Symbols: Explorations in Cosmology* (Pantheon, New York 1970) 125-139.

7. For example, see Leviticus 11.24-40; 14.7; 15.5-13, 18; Deuteronomy 23.10-11, etc.

8. The *Mishnah* contains twelve treatises on purifications, nuancing them according to degree of seriousness. Note Mark 7.1-5; Matthew 15.1-2; Luke 11.3-8. The extent to which water was needed for solemn meals can be seen in the account of the marriage feast at Cana in John 2.6f.

9. See Matthew 23.15, Acts 2.10; 6.5. The first undoubted evidence concerning the structure is in the *Mishnah* from around 90 A.D. See Beasley-Murray 23-25.

10. In the *Babylonian Talmud*, tractate Jebamot 47 a-b. See Delorme 28-29.

11. Thus Delorme 31. The influence of evolving Christian baptismal practice on the ritual codifications found later in the *Mishnah* and *Talmuds* cannot be wholly discounted.

12. See the *Mishnah*, tractate Mikwaoth, ch. 1. This seems to be the background for *Didache* 7: "Having first recited all these things, baptize in the Name of the Father, Son, and Holy Spirit in living water. But if you have no living water, then baptize in other water; and if you cannot in cold, then in warm . . . "

13. Tractate Mikwaoth, ch. 9. See chapter 2, note 56, p. 75.

14. Despite the apparent casualness of Philip's baptism of the eunuch (Acts 8.36-39), the account specifies that they went down *into* the water at the roadside and came *up out* of it.

15. Beasley-Murray 28.

16. E.g., Joachim Jeremias, *Die Kindertaufe in den ersten vier Jahrhunderten* (Vanderhoeck & Ruprecht, Göttingen 1958) 34-44. See Beasley-Murray 25-31 for a balanced critique of this opinion.

17. See Beasley-Murray 11-18; Delorme 35-48.

18. See Beasley-Murray 31-44; Delorme 48-60.

19. Matthew 3.11, Luke 3.16, perhaps with Malachi 3.1 in mind.

20. The synthesis, while final, was not unique. Psalms 21 and 56, for example, stress the need for ritual *and* moral purity in those taking part in worship in the temple. "The prophetic corrective of priestly religion has borne fruit": thus Beasley-Murray 9.

21. E.g., Justin's *Dialogue with Trypho* 80 (c. 160).

22. See Beasley Murray 7-10. Also Nils Dahl, "The Origin of Baptism," in *Interpretationes ad Vetus Testamentum pertinentes S. Mowinckel* (Forlaget Land og Kirke, Oslo 1955) 39.

23. Schnackenburg 8. See R. Fuller, "Christian Initiation in the New Testament," in *Made, Not Born. New Perspectives on*

Christian Initiation and the Catechumenate (University of Notre Dame Press, Notre Dame, Indiana 1976) 8-9.

24. Thus Beasley-Murray 64.

25. See Beasley-Murray 45-67 for a careful exegetical study of Jesus' baptism by John.

26. Beasley-Murray 72. On the Old Testament images, especially that of the cup of wrath to be drunk, which Jesus invokes along with that of baptism to convey the significance of his approaching passion, see 72-77.

27. Beasley-Murray 72. Tertullian, *On Baptism* 11, thinks these baptisms were certainly not "Christian" but were a continuation of John's: so too Chrysostom's homily 29 on John. Augustine, Peter Lombard, and Aquinas thought they were "Christian."

28. See Beasley-Murray 93-99.

29. Note the deeply semitic and Middle Eastern enthronement ritual aspects of this suggested by E. O. James, *Christian Myth and Ritual. A Historical Study* (J. Murray, London 1933) 100-101.

30. Beasley-Murray 16-17.

31. Note Acts 18.24–19.7, where those Paul baptizes and lays hands on seem to be followers of Jesus who had received only John's baptism.

32. Acts 10.44-47.

33. Acts 8.1-17.

34. Acts 2.37-38; 2.41; 8.12-13; 8.35-36; 16.14-15; 16.32-33; 18.8; 19.5. See W. F. Flemington, *The New Testament Doctrine of Baptism* (SPCK, London 1957) 49.

35. E.g., Acts 10.44; 11.14-15, where Peter is the apostolic agent.

36. See above, pp. 18-19.

37. E.g., Acts 8.4-17, where Philip's proclamation and baptisms among the Samaritans had to be completed by Peter and John as envoys of the Jerusalem community. In this

light, it may be significant that the account of Philip's baptism of the Ethiopian eunuch (Acts 8.26-39) mentions no pneumatic phenomena resulting from it except that Philip, not the eunuch, was "caught up" by the Spirit.

38. See Flemington 43-48 for a review and critique of such theories.

39. See Beasley-Murray 90-92; Schnackenburg 18-21.

40. Thus G. W. H. Lampe, *The Seal of the Spirit* (SPCK, London 1967) 81. See Beasley-Murray 234-235; Schnackenburg 89-91; Neunheuser, *Baptism and Confirmation*, trans. John Jay Hughes (Herder and Herder, New York 1964) 50-51. Flemington 67, regards the Pauline text as indicative of an actual anointing.

41. Thus Beasley-Murray 235; Lampe xix and passim.

42. One notes that the anointing of Jesus' corpse, after its washing in preparation for burial, had to be delayed due to the occurrence of Passover. The funeral bath was subject to Jewish law, but its procedures were not dissimilar to pagan baths for the same purpose. See G. Rowell, *The Liturgy of Christian Burial. An Introductory Survey of the Historical Development of Christian Burial Rites* (SPCK, London 1977) 1-18.

43. See Schnackenburg 205-206.

44. Also the *Epistle of Barnabas* 16:7-10; Justin's *Dialogue with Trypho* 116; Tertullian *On Baptism* 5-7.

45. Dahl 46.

46. *Pace* Lampe 136f, 159f.

Chapter Two

The Ritualization of Christian Initiation

Although liturgy is not primarily a text as is a letter or a book, nor does it necessarily involve words said, nonetheless texts consisting of words that were in fact said during a given liturgical act are often one's only clue to the act itself. In studying a liturgical complex such as that of Christian initiation, therefore, priority must be given to the actual texts of things said in a liturgical act, where these texts have survived. Failing such texts, one must fall back on a series of other data that are less directly related to the act itself. Sometimes the most salient of these will be ceremonial descriptions of the act, but where these too are absent one must entertain more oblique evidence such as pious or theological commentaries on the act or passing references to it. In all cases, however, the contemporary context of the act itself and of the evidence referring to it must be kept in mind lest one anachronize the data according to later understanding on the one hand, or atomize the data into an unintelligible state on the other.

Another methodological fact to remember is that liturgies are notoriously conservative. Because they are events in which large numbers of people take part, they resist change. Their evolution is normally slow; it was even slower prior to the invention of printing and the advent of high rates of literacy—both relatively modern phenomena. Given a choice between innovation and archaism, a liturgical tradition normally chooses the latter, especially when the choice involves a time or an event of high religious intensity for the tradition itself.[1] This does not mean that a liturgical structure will remain completely static. But it does mean that a Christian structure will cleave closer to its origins, in particular at the structural center, as it celebrates the *pascha*, for example. For all the development of the Christian eucharist over the past two millenia, its core still centers upon bread broken and wine poured out in a context of prayerful thanksgiving for all God has wrought, just as the earliest churches would have done in obedience to the exalted Lord's command, "Do this," at the Last Supper.

In the same way, for all the development of Christian initiation over the past two thousand years its core still centers upon proclamation, conversion, and baptism in its paschal fullness, just as the earliest churches would have done in obedience to the exalted Lord's command, "Go, teach, baptize, and make disciples of all nations." We have already seen that this complex set of rites was in place during the New Testament period not as a single simple act but as a continuum of articulated events already undergoing a rich if initial degree of development. While there is much that we do not know about this process in its early stages, we are never wholly without evidence of some kind. Even when the New Testament period ends and the postapostolic era begins, our evidence does not suddenly lapse on all fronts or take on a wholly different character.

One finds in the first seven chapters of the *Didache*, a primitive church order that began to be composed in Syria perhaps prior to 100 A.D.,[2] invaluable information on how converts are to be initiated. They are to be taught the "two ways" of life and death, a mode of teaching found in late Judaism and based perhaps on Deuteronomy 30.15f. They are to be baptized in the name of the Trinity in living water, if it is available; if not, any other water will do, and the act is to be done with all involved fasting. Having been thus prepared and baptized, the neophyte begins to live the Church's life, which is an ascetical one of fasting and prayer (chapter 8) and of the eucharist (chapters 9 and 10). The latter two chapters give us the first structure and texts of a Christian eucharist, which amount to a series of brief prayers of thanksgiving before and after a meal. As such, while it bases itself on the domestic Jewish meal hallowing the Sabbath, it adapts the meal to Christian purposes and fills it with new content. There is every reason to believe the same of its baptismal stipulations in chapters 1 through 7.

The pronouncedly Jewish character of the *Didache's* first ten chapters, which constitute the most primitive stratum of the document, seems to place it in a diaspora context such as was to be found in Antioch. All its structural precedents are Jewish—the two ways of teaching, the Kiddush-meal eucharist, and the ablutionary baptism.[3] This at least suggests that the *Didache* community belonged less to the hellenizing wing of early Christianity represented by Stephen, Philip, and Paul than to the more judaically inclined wing centered at Jerusalem until the death of James in 62 and the dispersal of Christians during the revolt of 66 to 70, when the destruction of the city took place at the hands of Roman troops.

Yet the document leaves many questions unanswered, not least of which is the role of the Holy Spirit in baptism. The pneumaticism of the *Didache* as a whole is not pronounced: its emphasis is rather upon ethical preparation for and life in an ascetical community founded upon faith in Jesus the Christ, servant of the Father in the line of David. It is Jesus who has made known the "life and knowledge" (chapter 9), "the knowledge and faith and immortality" (chapter 10) of the Father. In him the holy Name of the Father pitched its tent in our hearts, and by him all was created for the Father's Name. The Jewish emphasis on the "Name" is continued into baptism, for it is by baptism in Jesus' Name that one is hallowed to eat and drink the "spiritual (*pneumatike*) food and drink and eternal life" of the *eucharistia* (chapters 9 and 10). Baptism in Jesus' Name for this purpose is liturgically effected in water "in the Name of the Father and of the Son and of the Holy Spirit" (chapter 7), the context seeming to suggest that this is in fact a sacramental formula to be said as one pours water thrice on the head of the convert.

There is no mention of an anointing or hand-laying in connection with this baptism: the results of baptism are not completion rituals but fasting, prayer, and the "spiritual" food and drink of the eucharist. The term *pneumatike* in its eucharistic context clearly does not refer to the Holy Spirit but to the fact that this food and drink is distinct from that taken in the actual meal that would have occurred between the prayers of chapter 9 and those of chapter 10, the latter of which is prefaced by the direction: "After you are satisfied with food, give thanks thus . . . "

One discovers an initiatory pattern in the *Didache* in which there are not only no specifically pneumatic *gestes*, but the Holy Spirit is mentioned only in the baptismal formula itself. In the eucharistic prayers of chapters 9 and 10, moreover, the emphasis is on the power, might, and glory of the Father through Jesus Christ: the Spirit is not mentioned in any doxology or in either of the two petitions for the unity of the Church—prayers which may be seen as eucharistic protoepicleses. The pneumatology of the *Didache* is less developed in fact than that found in many New Testament works. This points at least to the great primitiveness of the document. It may also suggest that the initiatory structure it reports, condensed in chapters 1 through 7, is either enormously archaic, or relatively eccentric, or both. The fact that there is nothing *uniquely* Christian in the teaching of the first six chapters (with the possible exception of a loosening of dietary restrictions in chapter 6) might indicate that the *Didache* community described in the most primitive parts of the document was originally a group of Jewish sectaries, perhaps followers of John the Baptist and of ascetical bent, who only recently had adhered to the Exalted One. If so, their teaching preparatory for baptism would have had to change very little, and their repentance baptism would only have had to be more specific concerning in whose name it was done. Their ethos as an ascetical "baptist" group of messianic expectations shines through in the acclamations and a direction that conclude chapter 10: "Hosannah to the God of David. If anyone be holy, let him come: if anyone be not, let him repent. *Maran atha*. Amen. And let the prophets give thanks as they will."

What the *Didache* represents, at least in its most primitive portions, may thus not be so much the beginning of postapostolic church order as a witness to the early entry into Christianity of a particular group of sectaries strongly rooted in baptist and ascetical movements represented by John the Baptist, the Essenes, and the Qumran community. The ethos of chapters 1 through 10 seems more early New Testament (e.g., Acts 19.1-7) than postapostolic: its other parts appear to be later and may represent further stages in the Christian development of the group, especially as touching ministry and the "Lord's Day." And if the document is indeed Antiochean in origin, this could offer a clue to at least one sort of practice with which the famous martyr-bishop of Antioch, Ignatius (c. 35–c. 107), would have been familiar. This is, however, not the place to pursue such an hypothesis, for Ignatius' seven surviving letters to other churches emphasize points of ministry, eucharist, church unity, and the need to resist certain judaizing tendencies, but they say little about Christian initiation beyond insisting that the bishop should preside at baptism.[4]

ABORIGINAL PATTERNS: EAST SYRIA AND THE GRAECO-LATIN WEST

From the allusive evidence of the New Testament and the highly archaic, perhaps eccentric, evidence contained in the *Didache* it is clear that initiatory practice was pluralistic and developing by the beginning of the second century. But the same evidence does not yet allow one to speak with confidence of the settling in of definite patterns beyond the water bath. What is contained in these early documents, however, when taken together with second and early third century evidence of a more definitely liturgical character, does reveal two emergent patterns of initiatory ritualization which, given the conservatism of liturgical evidence, may perhaps extend back into the period of the later books of the New Testament itself. If this is true, then one may refer to these patterns as liturgically aboriginal.

The first pattern of initiatory ritualization may be detected in primitive East Syrian and Armenian liturgical sources—namely, in the Syriac *Acts of Thomas*, the *Didascalia Apostolorum*, and the rites of the *Armenian Ordo* (finally compiled in the third to the fifth centuries).[5] What unites these sources is their profound archaism and their rooting in a strongly semitic cultural-linguistic milieu in the hinterland east of the Greek-speaking coastal areas of Palestine and western Syria. The sequence of baptism revealed in the earliest stratum of these documents is 1) an *anointing* with olive oil (*meshha*) on the head; 2) the water bath by triple immersion in the Name of the Trinity; and 3) the *eucharist*.[6] At a later date, perhaps in the fourth century, to the "messianic" anointing of the head before the water bath is added a "healing" anointing of the whole body, and a formal blessing of the oil begins the service.[7] Only subsequent to these additions will another anointing after the water bath be included, this with *chrisma*,[8] apparently as a result of influence stemming from the Greek-speaking churches along the seacoast. The first anointing is called *rushma* (sign or mark), the later anointing with chrism *hatma* (seal).[9]

One may sense something of the religious sentiment that pervaded this archaic semitic set of rites from the reports of baptisms contained in chapters 27 and 132 of the *Acts of Thomas*. In the first of these it is said that the apostle

". . . went up and stood at the edge of the cistern, and poured oil upon their heads, and said: 'Come, holy name of the Messiah; come, power of grace, which art from on high; come, perfect mercy; come, exalted gift; come, sharer of the blessing; come, revealer of hidden mysteries; come, mother of seven houses, whose rest was in the eighth house; come, messenger of reconciliation . . . ; come, Spirit of holiness, and purify their reins and hearts.' And he baptized them in the Name of the Father and of the Son and of the Spirit of holiness . . . And when it dawned and was morning, he broke the Eucharist."[10]

In the second instance, the baptizer begins with an instruction on baptism which quickly becomes an ecstatic doxology glorifying the power of baptism:

"And when he had said these things, he cast oil upon their heads and said: 'Glory to thee, thou beloved fruit [i.e., the oil, *meshha*].' And he spake, and they brought a large vat, and he baptized them in the name of the Father and the Son and the Spirit of holiness. And when they were baptized and had put on their clothes, he brought bread and wine."[11]

From these two reports, and from the rest of the group of documents that forms their context, it seems that the theory undergirding archaic Syrian baptismal initiation centered on the Jordan event as type and emphasized the manifestation there of Jesus as prophet, priest, and king—the Anointed One, the *Messiah-Christos*. So too the Christian in baptism, as in 1 Peter 2.9. The act is a "birth" (Psalm 2.7, John 3.3-5), the water a womb. But the emphasis is on the anointing: "In the process of ritualization, therefore, it was the anointing that became, in Syria, the first and only visible gesture for the central event at Christ's baptism: his revelation as the Messiah-King through the descent of the Spirit."[12]

The second, more western, pattern of initiatory ritualization can be sensed initially in Justin's *First Apology* and viewed more fully about a generation later in the *Apostolic Tradition* of Hippolytus and in Tertullian's *On Baptism*, two works which are contemporary with each other at the beginning of the third century. Of this group of documents, the *Apology* (c. 150) and *Apostolic Tradition* (c. 215) are associated with the Greek-speaking church of Rome; *On Baptism* (c. 200) with the Latin-speaking church of Carthage. As such, they are at least contemporary with, or earlier than, the Syrian texts already mentioned.

Justin, who was born in hellenized Palestine close to the time of Ignatius' death, addressed his *Apology* to a non-Christian audience. In chapters 61 and 65 of the work he recounts in very general terms, therefore, "the manner in which we dedicated ourselves to God when we were made new through Christ":

"As many as are persuaded and believe that these things which we teach and describe are true, and undertake to live accordingly, are taught to pray and ask God, while fasting, for the forgiveness of their sins; and we pray and fast with them. Then they are led to a place where there is water, and they are reborn after the manner of rebirth by which we also were reborn: for they are then washed in the water in the name of the Father and Lord God of all things, and of our Saviour Jesus Christ, and of the Holy Spirit . . . [After that] we lead him to those who are called brethren, where they are assembled, and make common prayer fervently for ourselves, for him that has been enlightened, and for all men everywhere,[13] that, embracing the truth, we may be found in our lives good and obedient citizens, and also attain to everlasting salvation."[14]

The eucharist follows, beginning with the kiss of peace followed by bread and wine being brought to the table for the presider to give thanks over.

The initiatory description in Justin's *Apology* is general, structurally sequential, and meant to secure good public relations. It is religious advertisement broadcast with a certain reticence—not primarily a theological treatise, a code of ceremonial directions, or a sermon to the baptized. In this light, what liturgical information it does provide in passing, while hardly exhaustive, is of high significance. One notices, for example, a more detailed structural transition from the water bath to the eucharist than has been suggested in any prior document. From a "place where there is water" the newly baptized are led "to those who are called brethren, where they are assembled." The place of baptism is separate, perhaps even at some distance from the place where the assembly is gathered: the brethren apparently do not take part in the events at the "place where there is water," perhaps due to the nudity of the candidates, but remain in assembly elsewhere awaiting the arrival of the newly baptized once they have been groomed and dressed after immersion. At this point the brethren assembled receive them with "common, fervent prayer" before the eucharist begins. This is the earliest clear evidence for what will later be called the prayer of the faithful, a set of general intercessions for Church and world only the baptized Faithful were empowered to say, and which connected the service of the Word to the eucharistic banquet. In Justin's *Apology* it appears as the first act of the newly baptized as they enter the ranks of the *fideles*. It too implies that the Faithful had been in assembly during the baptisms, probably at a Word service or vigil that continued until the arrival of the baptismal party. Even Lampe, who resists the notion that baptism included any rites other than the water bath until much later, feels compelled to admit the probability that, at the reception of the newly baptized in Justin's *Apology*, "the presiding bishop may have received the converts into the fellowship with a sign of blessing; it would be rather surprising if he did not do so."[15]

What this reception of the newly baptized into the assembly of the Faithful in fact amounted to in the Greek and Latin west can be seen in Tertullian's *On Baptism* and Hippolytus' *Apostolic Tradition* a generation or so after Justin's time. Given the conservative nature of liturgical practice it is very dubious that vast structural innovation took place in this interval: both Tertullian and Hippolytus were in addition among the most conservative of men. Not only was neither a warm host to novelty, but both actively opposed it in their writings, and Tertullian at least finally went into schism over it. Novelty in basics such as baptism and eucharist strikes both authors as a weakening of that apostolic tradition which secures fidelity to the gospel. Hippolytus begins the *Apostolic Tradition* inveighing against "ignorant men," by which he seems to mean certain bishops and presbyters of the Roman church. Tertullian opens *On Baptism* with an assault on "a certain female viper from the Cainite sect, who recently spent some time here, [and] carried off a good number with her exceptionally pestilential doctrine, making a particular point of demolishing baptism."[16] He continues, giving a sense of the way baptism was perceived in the context of his place and time:

"There is indeed nothing which so hardens men's minds as the simplicity of God's works as they are observed in action, compared with the magnificence promised in their effects. So in this case too, because with such complete simplicity, without display, without any unusual equipment, and (not least) without anything to pay, a man is sent down into the water, is washed to the accompaniment of very few words, and comes up little or no cleaner than he was, his attainment to eternity is regarded as beyond belief. On the contrary, if I mistake not, the solemn ceremonies, or even the secret rites, of idolatry work up for themselves credence and prestige by pretentious magnificence and by the fees that are charged. O that poverty-striken unbelief, which denies to God his characteristic attributes, simplicity and power."[17]

What details Tertullian's treatise and Hippolytus' church order specify concerning baptismal initiation over and above those mentioned in Justin's apologetic work are thus not so much due to the time separating them as to the differences in their literary genres. Justin's was meant primarily for external, Tertullian's and Hippolytus' for internal, consumption. If one takes all three together as witnesses to a basically common ritual pattern whose continuing ritual development is less in basic structure than in nuance, then a structure and a corresponding theory different from that of East Syria becomes evident.

The structure of initiation in this early Graeco-Latin context involves 1) stress on *instruction preparatory for baptism*;[18] 2) an *anointing* with exorcized oil after Satan has been renounced;[19] 3) the *water bath* by triple immersion in the Name of the Trinity; 4) an *anointing with chrism* (Tertullian) or *oil of thanksgiving* (Hippolytus);[20] 5) a *hand-laying* by the bishop with prayer invoking the Holy Spirit, joined in Hippolytus with a final anointing on the forehead with consecrated oil as a "sealing";[21] 6) the *eucharist*.[22] Tertullian assigns messianic effects to the postbaptismal anointing with chrism.

The theory of early Graeco-Latin baptismal initiation stresses prebaptismal preparation through instruction together with ascetical formation and exorcism due perhaps to the increasing number of gentile converts outside Syria and Palestine. A second stress is upon acts that take place during the reception of the newly baptized into the assembly before the eucharist begins—namely, the postbaptismal anointing(s) and hand-laying by the bishop as he invokes the Holy Spirit. These two stresses have the effect of creating a liturgical symmetry centering upon the water bath itself. And while Greek and Latin services a century later begin to focus on the water bath as a death and burial,[23] these three earlier sources do not emphasize this aspect. Their ethos is more controlled by the notion of birth and cleansing for the remission of sins.[24]

Perhaps the gentile background of so many Greek and Latin converts later led to an increasing emphasis on the water bath as a death to all that they had previously been. In any case, the major act in the whole initiatory process is the baptism itself; the pneumatic and consecratory anointing with oil after it is its outcome. But this outcome is of high pastoral importance, as may be seen in the evolution of a liturgical reception of the newly baptized convert, who has now left the powerful cultural context of his or her former life, and has entered into a new life lived in new surroundings. Far from leaving the neophytes to shift for themslves because everything had in fact been theologically accomplished in the water bath, our three sources show that the newly baptized are received into full communion with the Church by a series of hospitable acts—clothing, solemn public prayer, chrismations, hand-layings, kisses of peace, and finally admission to the common table of the eucharist. This pastoral-liturgical context is that within which all the events after the water bath must be interpreted: they cannot be sundered from their pastoral context, then be liturgically isolated from each other and still be expected to make complete sense in themselves. Yet, as we shall see, this is what happened as the whole initiatory continuum became fragmented in later centuries, making it possible for theologians and polemicists to exploit each of its isolated parts for various ends.

When one compares what appears to be the two aboriginal patterns of initiatory ritualization in East Syria and the Graeco-Latin west, several factors deserve comment.

First, the East Syrian emphasis on anointing *before* the water bath as the pneumatic and messianic event *par excellence* both reflected and retained many of the eschatological and even eccentric characteristics of the gospel at the very core of Christian life. This ethos is marked in the earliest Syrian sources we have sketched. It is also evident in the subsequent evolution of Syrian church order, folk piety, liturgy, and asceticism, giving rise to a wholly distinct Christian idiom. To note but one example of this: if Latin monasticism assumed a quasi-urban form that would teach barbarized western Europe the civil arts, and if Egyptian monasticism adopted an almost military form of discipline that would unwittingly provide shock troops for all sides in the coming centuries of rancorous doctrinal dispute, then Syrian monks would be the spirit-haunted holy men of ferocious individuality whose incredible feats (such as sitting atop pillars for forty years) astonished and unsettled the Graeco-Latin world.[25] These last were the born-again heroes of a folk Christianity that had no equal except in Egypt: both constituted a populist idiom that shrank from the urban idioms of Rome and, later, Constantinople, especially after the Council of Chalcedon in 451. If one had been born into the eschatological kingdom of the Messiah-King and assimilated to him in the Spirit of God as an anointed one oneself, then what had one to do with prince and patriarch by mere law established? Syro-Christian "radicalism," in this sense, largely withdrew into the so-called non-Chalcedonian churches after the fifth century, where it has remained an idiom of almost impenetrable difficulty for both Byzantine and Roman orthodoxy ever since.

Second, while the ethos of East Syrian baptismal patterns is perhaps more consecratory than initiatory, and as such may be said to be more native to the gospels of Mark–Matthew and John, it would be too much to conclude that this ethos was more "original" than that of the Graeco-Latin churches. Baptismal polity was both pluralistic and evolving even within the New Testament period itself. The dates of our liturgical sources both east and west furthermore do not permit us to claim a chronological priority for one pattern over the other. For a variety of reasons, not all of which are theological, primitive East Syria stressed the birth imagery of John 3, together with pneumatic and messianic elements and interpretations as a rule: the Graeco-Latin west came to emphasize, also for a variety of reasons, the death-bath imagery of Romans 6, together with purificatory and instructional elements and interpretations as a rule. One must emphasize, however, that these contrasting stresses are neither absolute nor mutually exclusive. Even in the early Syrian sources already mentioned, the purificatory notion of baptism as a forgiveness of sins is not absent.[26] Nor are the notes of messianic consecration, charism, or birth absent in Tertullian and Hippolytus.[27] And while the notion of messianic consecration does seem to fade in western texts, the notions of the gifts of the Spirit, birth, and regeneration remain strong. An example of this may be seen in the fifth century inscription, perhaps composed by Leo the Great (c. 461), in the Lateran baptistry:

"Here is born in Spirit-soaked fertility
a brood destined for another City,
begotten by God's blowing
and borne upon this torrent
by the Church their virgin mother.
Reborn in these depths they reach for heaven's realm,
the born-but-once unknown by felicity.
This spring is life that floods the world,
the wounds of Christ its awesome source.
Sinner sink beneath this sacred surf
that swallows age and spits up youth.
Sinner here scour sin away down to innocence,
for they know no enmity who are by
one font, one Spirit, one faith made one.
Sinner shudder not at sin's kind and number,
for those born here are holy."[28]

Third, within the Graeco-Latin patterns reported by Tertullian and Hippolytus at almost the same time, one notes an important difference: Tertullian knows only one anointing after the water bath (that with chrism) and a hand-laying[29] while Hippolytus speaks of yet another one which follows the bishop's laying hands on the neophyte's head. In both, the first anointing takes place as the baptized *emerges* from the bath: since Hippolytus makes it clear that the neophyte is still naked, the implication is that the baptismal party is still in Justin's "place where there is water." After this, Hippolytus specifies that the anointed ones then dry themselves, put on their clothes, "and after this let them be together in the assembly." There, the neophytes must have been presented to the assembly, and their reception into its midst is the setting for the bishop's laying hands on them with prayer invoking the Holy Spirit "in the holy Church"; whereupon the bishop again lays his hand on each head and anoints the forehead, perhaps with his thumb in the sign of the cross. The neophyte, whose baptism and anointing apart from the assembly has now been "sealed" in the assembly's midst, is then received into it with the kiss of peace, being greeted for the first time as a member of the Faithful ("The Lord be with you") and responding as one in his or her first utterance as a member of the Faithful ("And with your Spirit"). The eucharist ensues.

The difference between Tertullian and Hippolytus on this point may be due to the fact that it was not to the former's purpose to go into what happened after the water bath beyond the anointing immediately following it. But this argument from silence cannot be pressed since other major churches outside that of North Africa, namely, those of Greek-speaking West Syria and Palestine, know Tertullian's pattern rather than that of Hippolytus.[30] Only the churches of Milan[31] and Rome[32] follow Hippolytus' pattern. Other

Latin churches of the west seem originally to have observed the practice of North Africa and the Greek west: the north Italian *Bobbio Missal* (c. 700), for example, while hybridized with Roman and Milanese elements, knows only one postbaptismal anointing with chrism, and the Irish *Stowe Missal* (c. 800) has two apparent anointings after baptism, the second of which may in fact be only an alternate exorcism for the oil.[33]

In view of this structural variation, which appears in the west by the beginning of the third century, one may further specify the early patterns of initiatory ritualization. There is 1) the East Syrian pattern, which emphasizes an anointing before the water bath but originally had no anointing after it; 2) the Graeco-Latin type of North Africa, West Syria, and Palestine, which knows one anointing with chrism after the water bath; and 3) the Graeco-Latin pattern of the Rome–Milan axis, which used an anointing of an exorcistic character prior to the water bath and either two anointings with hand-laying (Hippolytus) or one anointing plus a "spiritual seal" (Ambrose) after it. Although Ambrose of Milan never actually calls the "spiritual seal" either an anointing or a hand-laying, he associates its meaning with the gifts of the Holy Spirit. That this involved an anointing with *myron* (as Ambrose calls the oil of the first post-baptismal anointing), hand-laying, and signation on the forehead seems probable. The witness of Hippolytus, together with that of the earliest full Roman texts in the *Gelasian Sacramentary*, suggest that this was Roman practice at Ambrose's time. Had Ambrose departed from Roman usage on this point he surely would have mentioned it, as he did the non-Roman custom at Milan of washing the feet of the newly baptized after they emerged from the font.[34]

The foregoing has attempted to do no more than sketch the genesis of the main patterns of baptismal initiation which seem to underlie all subsequent liturgical developments in the major churches east and west. Its purpose has been to clarify basic trends rather than to be exhaustive in detail so that several matters that later become intensely problematic, especially in western Catholic practice, may be thrown into bold relief.

Anointing with oil in connection with baptism, for example, is witnessed in the very earliest stages of the ritualization process. Far from being a late addition of secondary or tertiary theological importance, the primitive East Syrian sources, steeped in the semitic imagery of the gospels, seem to have placed the anointing at least on a level of importance with the water bath itself. In this there seems to be no hint of the practice being regarded as an innovation. Rather, the motive for it appears to be one of remaining faithful to the substantial meaning of Jesus' baptism as reported by the gospels themselves. The Baptist baptized in water: Jesus came to baptize with Holy Spirit. The scene at the Jordan culminates not in Jesus' descent into the water but in the descent of the Spirit upon him, designating him the Anointed One of prophecy. No unambiguous early *ritual* of baptism after the *Didache*, whose eccentric archaism we have noted, is without an anointing at some point. The least that can be said is that anointing seems to be the earliest *ritual* act associated with the water to be emphasized, earlier even than *liturgical* hand-laying—mentioned first by Hippolytus and bracketed by *two* postbaptismal anointings.

Indeed, the usage described by Hippolytus, when interpreted in context with his pneumatic ecclesiology ("in the Holy Spirit in the holy Church"), appears to be a rather sophisticated combination of acts—so sophisticated indeed as to be unique. The newly baptized is publicly received in the assembly by the communion gesture of the bishop's hand being laid on his or her head[35] in conjunction with an invocation of the Holy Spirit *and* a final anointing with consecrated oil. The neophyte's whole conversion process and baptism is thus "sealed" in public with a mark on the forehead. Christian fellowship in the fullest and most unqualified sense is the result: it is life "in the Holy Spirit in the holy Church." A web of intimately articulated meanings has been matched with a multiplicity of closely coordinated acts. The liturgical genius of this arrangement is remarkable. Yet its genius consists in the mutual dependency of each of its parts: like an ecological system, it is robust only to the extent that its parts remain both whole and in vital harmony. Disrupt that harmony and the whole system mutates.

One can contend that the Hippolytan baptismal synthesis of meaning and rites constitutes or at least witnesses the genesis of Roman initiatory practice. More particularly, in the gradual disruption of the synthesis in its postbaptismal parts can be traced the evolution of peculiarly Roman difficulties with its own initiatory polity. Not only does this disruption (so gradual in its taking place as to have been at no one time fully perceptible) produce the separate rite of hand-laying and anointing that came to be known in later centuries as the sacrament of confirmation, but this one symptom of the disruption more than any other factor produces a shifting perception of the water bath itself.

While doubts about the Romanness of Hippolytus' liturgy have been expressed by some,[36] they have not overcome the tradition that associates the author of the *Apostolic Tradition* with the City.[37] Be this as it may, the Hippolytan initiatory pattern emerges as the only one indisputably attested in the liturgy of the City by the time of the eighth century *Gelasian Sacramentary* and its ceremonial companionpiece, the *Ordo Romanus XI*.[38] No plausible explanation of subsequent Roman initiatory practice can avoid beginning with Hippolytus-based initiatory patterns found in these two later documents. "In these two books," says Neunheuser, "we find the oldest form of the baptismal liturgy in the Roman Church which is preserved in the preconciliar rite for adult baptism."[39]

ROMAN ADAPTATION OF THE INITIATORY PATTERN OF HIPPOLYTUS

In approaching the three Roman documents it is well to remember that one is dealing with two initiatory *orders*. *Apostolic Tradition* (hereafter referred to as *AT*) represents, at the latest, a second or early third century order of initiation in its chapters 16-22: the *Gelasian Sacramentary* (*Gel*) and *Ordo Romanus XI* (*OR*) together represent a sixth to eighth century order for the same purpose. Both orders embrace more than just the baptismal rites themselves: both orders begin with the enrollment of a convert in the formation program meant to prepare one for the baptismal rites when these were normally celebrated at the vigil of Easter and at Pentecost.[40] For the sake of clarity, each of the major stages in the initiatory process will be examined in sequence, comparing the two orders at each stage.

Enrollment

AT says only that those who come forward for the first time to "hear the word" should be presented to the teachers of the community privately so that their motives can be examined and vouched for by "those who bring them." Admission to "hear the word" is not a mere formality: whole classes of people— such as pimps, teachers of pagan philosophy, pagan priests, makers of idols or amulets, and men with concubines—are not to be accepted into this class of learners, or catechumens, unless they first forsake their modes of life. The crux of this admission procedure has nothing to say about the intentions of the applicant: it is his manner of living that is to be ascertained and, apparently, nothing more. From this point on, the applicant, if accepted into the catechumenate, will be expected to begin living in a manner befitting a Christian—a manner that will be gradually molded by the teaching, moral support, prayer, example, and ritual patterns of the Christian community itself. From this moment, the convert is regarded no longer as a pagan but as an incipient Christian.[41]

The later Roman documents, from an era when the Christianization of society was all but complete, seem not nearly so pastoral on the matter of enrollment of catechumens as *AT*. If the ritual of the act is more detailed, the situation it responds to seems more remote. Yet underneath its rather stiffened symbolism one can still detect the memory of a time when coping with highly diverse applicants for Christian initiation was high on the list of pastoral priorities. The rite for making a catechumen, in fact, no longer appears in *Gel* at the beginning of the liturgy of the catechumenate but among texts to be used in special circumstances. Its introductory rubric reads more like a gesture to tradition than the introduction to a pastorally vivid event: "When you receive one of heathen upbringing, first you catechize him with divine words and teach him how he must live after he has come to the knowledge of the truth. Then you make him a catechumen: you blow into his face and make the sign of the cross upon his forehead: you lay a hand upon his head and say . . . "[42] Two prayers for the applicant follow, then "the medicine of salt" is given the applicant as a symbolic preservative from corruption; he signs himself and a prayer of blessing concludes the event. There is no mention of an examination of motives or of supporting witness being sought of sponsors, who are not mentioned. The pastoral scrutiny of *AT* has become a ritual with a pronounced exorcistic tone.

The Catechumenate

AT speaks only generically about the details of the catechumenate. Its length is normally three years, but this is flexible depending on the earnestness and perseverance of the catechumen. The format of the catechetical sessions with the teacher is, however, mentioned:

"Each time the teacher finishes his instruction let the catechumens pray by themselves apart from the faithful. But after the prayer is finished the catechumens shall not give the kiss of peace, for their kiss is not yet pure. After the prayer let the teacher lay hands upon them and dismiss them. Whether the teacher be an ecclesiastic or a layman let him do the same."[43]

While a great deal of evidence on the *content* of early prebaptismal catechesis survives,[44] this is rare information on the *form* taken by catechetical sessions in the early church. It suggests that instruction did not take place in a classroom setting, pursuing exclusively intellectual matters in an abstract manner. Rather, it seems to have taken place at least within a prayer context: it may have assumed a more pronounced liturgical or quasi-liturgical setting, perhaps that of an actual service of the Word. This may even have been the origin of such a service—involving reverent reading of biblical lessons, an expounding of their meaning by the teacher in homiletic fashion, formal petitionary prayer, concluding with a laying of hands by the teacher and dismissal. *AT* strongly implies that so similar is the form in which catechumens are instructed to the form in which the baptized Faithful are instructed each Sunday before the eucharist that catechumens, being familiar with it, must be cautioned by their teachers that their prayer is not that of the Faithful and must therefore not conclude with the kiss of peace. *AT* seems to be as concerned to differentiate two quite similar kinds of formation events as to assure that the catechumenal event prepare its participants for the worship event, different in quality if not in kind, into which they will enter fully at their baptism. The catechumens' prayerful worship, is, as it were, the type of which the Faithful's is the antitype and consummation. One is formed in the gospel not only by learning but by worship as well, the two being articulated in a balanced continuum.

Of all this there is nothing in the later Roman documents. This does not mean that the catechumenate was unknown or had completely disappeared by the sixth century. As we shall see, a lenten liturgical structure for catechumens in proximate preparation for baptism is present in these texts and is of considerable complexity. But these texts have by the sixth century evolved beyond the rather general church order genre of *AT* and have become liturgical books in the strictest sense. They contain almost exclusively things to be said (*Gel*) or done (*OR*) at the altar. Thus the less formal considerations of catechesis are absent from them until such time as catechumens begin to enter the last and most public stage of baptismal preparation during the final weeks before the Easter season.

Election and Public Scrutiny

AT specifies that

> ". . . when they are chosen who are set apart to receive baptism let their life be examined whether they lived piously as catechumens, whether they honored the widows, whether they visited the sick, whether they have fulfilled every good work. If those who bring them bear witness to them that they have done thus, then let them hear the gospel. Moreover, from the day they are chosen, let a hand be laid upon them and let them be exorcized daily."[45]

From this it is clear once again that the main weight of early catechetical formation rested on how well a catechumen had begun to live his or her faith rather than on how much intellectual knowledge about it had been mastered. The witness of this was, it seems, less the teacher than the catechumen's sponsor, the one who had originally recommended him or her for admission to the catechumenate in the first place, and who no doubt had assumed the responsibility of overseeing the catechumen's mode of life ever since.[46] When this had reached a level of constancy, combined with a certain ease in clearly perceived practical ways, the catechumen was "set apart" to receive baptism. The manner of doing this is not stated, but since from that point the catechumen is daily to have a hand laid on him and be exorcized daily, the presumption is that the setting apart as well as the hand-laying and exorcism are public affairs within the community. The catechumen comes at this point into the public forum of the church's worship life, no longer abiding on its edge. The church's proximate preparation for the *pascha* seems by Hippolytus' time to have begun to expand beyond a few days' fast because of the introduction into it of increasing numbers of converts making ready to pass through the waters of death and rebirth as the Lord himself did in the "baptism" with which he had to be baptized. This expansion of the preparatory fast in favor of those about to die and be raised in him is the genesis of Lent. It was a time less of negative penitence than of positive preparation for the whole Church to relive and thus renew its own conversion in the passage of its catechumens into life in Christ through baptism.

Gel and *OR* do no more than specify in much greater liturgical detail Hippolytus' general description of how catechumens are chosen, examined, have hands laid on them and are exorcized. From the end of the fourth century at least it was Roman practice to elect at the beginning of Lent senior catechumens for the sacraments of initiation.[47] The Roman documents deal mainly with public events that are beginning to take place involving the elected catechumens on the third, fourth, and fifth Sundays of Lent, and on the morning of Holy Saturday. According to *Gel*, on three lenten Sundays with the whole community present the catechumens are examined in a rite known as the "scrutiny."[48] This rite is nothing less than a formal act of *catechesis* done now no longer apart from the community but with its participation and in its solemn presence. Its liturgical form and detail should not confuse one. As John the Deacon explained to Senarius around 500:

"*Catechesis* is the Greek word for instruction. [The catechumen] is instructed through the Church's ministry, by the blessing of one laying his hand [on his head], that he may know who he is and who he will be: in other words, that from being one of the damned he becomes holy, from unrighteousness he appears as righteous, and finally, from being a servant he becomes a son: so that a man whose first parentage brought him perdition is restored by the gift of a second parentage, and becomes the possessor of a father's inheritance. He receives therefore exsufflation [blowing] and exorcism . . . so that being delivered from the power of darkness he may be translated to the kingdom of glory of the love of God. . . . The catechumen receives blessed salt also, to signify that just as all flesh is kept healthy by salt, so the mind which is drenched and weakened by the waves of this world is held steady by the salt of wisdom and of the preaching of the word of God. . . . This then is achieved by frequent laying on of the hand, and by the blessing of his Creator . . . "[49]

Here one may see once again that catechesis was not mainly notional instruction on the subjective level but active formation on the objective level as well, involving prayer, hand-laying, exorcism, fasting, and tasting salt. The lenten scrutinies in *Gel* and *OR* are thus at base major acts of catechesis in which the whole community begins now to take part. Unlike earlier levels of catechesis, these do not address themselves to the more personal and subjective aspects of a catechumen's conversion process. The scrutinies presume that an elected catechumen has reached a further maturity of personal conversion: they begin to make that conversion the public property of the community as the catechumen approaches the sacraments of initiation at Easter. The Church claims that conversion as its own and gives itself to the catechumen in return. The liturgical scrutinies of Lent are therefore both in whole and in each of their parts salient dimensions of the whole catechetical process by which one is formed for full participation in a life of faith.[50]

The elements of the lenten scrutinies for the elect differ from those of previous catechetical sessions more in the degree of their fullness and solemnity than in kind. The elect are signed with the cross, hands are extended over or laid on their heads; they pray, listen to lessons from scripture, are prayed for, exorcized, and dismissed. On the fourth Sunday of Lent in addition to these things the elect are "given," with the greatest solemnity possible, the four Gospels (each one of which is briefly explained to them); the Creed (which is chanted for them to hear in both Latin and Greek, harking back to the time when the church of the City was actually bilingual); and the Lord's Prayer.[51]

On Holy Saturday morning the elect meet together as catechumens for the last time. Here they are "catechized" by undergoing a final exorcism; they renounce Satan, are anointed with the "oil of exorcism" which has been blessed along with the chrism the preceding Holy Thursday, and recite the Creed which they have memorized since hearing it in the fourth scrutiny. They kneel for prayer, and are then dismissed, being told to go home "and await the hour when the grace of God in baptism shall be able to enfold you."[52]

Sacramental Initiation

Hippolytus also has the elect meet with their bishop in the same manner:

"And on the Sabbath the bishop shall assemble those who are to be baptized in one place, and shall bid them all to pray and bow the knee. And laying his hands on them he shall exorcise every evil spirit. . . . And when he has finished exorcizing, let him breathe [or blow] on their faces and seal their foreheads and ears and noses and then let him raise them up. And they shall spend all the night in vigil, reading the scriptures to them and instructing them."[53]

OR says that the vigil service of Easter begins with a "blessing of the candle," after which follow "the lessons belonging to the day."[54] *Gel* gives eleven lessons from the Old Testament for the vigil, each with a prayer following.[55] Then the bishop, his clergy, and the elect proceed to the place of baptism while a litany is sung. There the bishop consecrates the waters of the font by invoking God to send the power of his Holy Spirit into it for the sacred purpose about to be accomplished.[56]

Hippolytus directs that when the baptismal party arrives at the place of baptism the bishop prays over the water. Then the elect strip, loosening their hair and removing all jewelry, lest anyone "go down into the water having any alien object with them." Each candidate next renounces Satan and is anointed by a presbyter with the "oil of exorcism" saying: "Let all evil spirits depart far from thee"—an act which the later Roman documents moved to the preceding morning, probably for logistical reasons, as we have seen. Then each candidate descends naked into the water where another presbyter and a deacon await. It seems that the presbyter in the font, beneath the bishop's gaze, lays his hand on the candidate and asks whether he or she believes first in the Father, then in the Son, and then in the Holy Spirit in the holy Church. Each time the candidate responds "I believe," the assisting deacon immerses him or her. After the third immersion the candidate comes up out of the water and is immediately anointed, still wet and naked, with the "oil of thanksgiving" (probably by the same presbyter who administered the first anointing) with the words, "I anoint thee with holy oil in the Name of Jesus Christ."[57] The newly baptized are then dried and dressed, "and after this let them be together in the assembly."[58]

Gel follows exactly the same order for the actual baptisms, but an expansion has occurred in the words which accompany the anointing after the baptism.

On coming out of the font the neophyte, or *infans*, is signed on the crown of the head with chrism by the presbyter, who says: "The Almighty God, the Father of our Lord Jesus Christ, who has made thee to be regenerated of water and the Holy Spirit, and has given thee remission of all thy sins, himself anoints thee with the chrism of salvation in Christ Jesus unto eternal life."[59] *OR* notes that the newly baptized are then dried. The bishop goes to a throne placed either in the *ecclesia fontis* (the baptistry itself) or in another hall sometimes called the *consignatorium*. Here the neophytes are solemnly robed with stole, chasuble, chrismal cloth, and given ten coins. Thus arrayed, they stand in a circle before the bishop as he prays for the gift of the sevenfold grace of the Holy Spirit, an invocation with which he is said to "confirm" them.[60] They are then signed by the bishop with chrism (*ad consignandum*) on their foreheads in the sign of the cross as he greets them for the first time as Christians, and afterwards they all enter the church in procession as a litany is chanted. The bishop ascends to his throne and intones *gloria in excelsis*, with which the Easter eucharist begins.[61]

AT describes the same events in simpler form. The baptismal party enters the church after the neophytes are dressed, and here before all the Faithful the bishop lays his hand upon the neophytes and invokes the grace of the Holy Spirit upon them. He then anoints them on the forehead as he lays his hand again on their heads, saying: "I anoint thee with holy oil in God the Father Almighty and Christ Jesus and the Holy Ghost." Their baptism thus "sealed" publicly in the assembly of the Faithful, the neophytes are greeted by the bishop and receive from him the kiss of peace. "Thenceforth," says Hippolytus, "they shall pray together with all the people. But they shall not previously pray with the faithful before they have undergone these things. And after the prayers, let them give the kiss of peace."[62] The Easter eucharist follows.

Summary

There can be no doubt that fundamental samenesses exist between the initiatory rites described in the early third century by Hippolytus and that contained in the earliest full Roman liturgical documents of the sixth to the eighth centuries. The three sources represent what is most probably a single liturgy in stages of evolution: *Gel* and *OR*, being later and much more detailed, give the polity its distinctive set, stamping it as uniquely Roman among all the other initiatory liturgies that were evolving concurrently in different ways both east and west. Yet, as with all evolution, differences between prior and subsequent stages of evolution are apparent. Attention to these differences often allows the interpreter to sense the direction in which the evolutionary flow is tending, and in the case of our three documents this flow can perhaps be summarized as follows.

First, both *AT* and *Gel–OR* exhibit the same initiatory sequence from the point of becoming a catechumen through the baptismal eucharist of Easter. This sameness is not only in general but often in detail as well. There exists no major discrepancy between the two sequences, yet *Gel–OR* is more developed and detailed both in the literary exposition of the whole sequence and in liturgical particulars, such as the scrutiny rituals.

Second, in both sets of documents physical *gestes* touch the initiate at every significant point throughout the initiation sequence. It amounts to a highly tactile choreography encompassing repeated hand-layings, feedings with salt (the "sacrament" of the catechumen),[63] the eucharistic bread and wine and milk and honey mixed,[64] signings with the cross on the forehead, anointings with the oil of exorcism and the oil of thanksgiving or chrism, and clothing in new garments. Yet in *Gel–OR* these are becoming more formalized and restricted to the major ritual events of the solemn scrutinies and the actual sacraments of initiation.

Third, the initiatory structure reaches its highest emotional and liturgical peak in the presentation and reception of the newly baptized within the gathered assembly of the Faithful. This event must originally have halted the long paschal vigil, resulting in a huge surge of sentiment among the whole gathering as the neophytes—still damp, oily, fragrant, and dressed in new garments—were presented to the church by its bishop. The event is still structurally discernible in *Gel–OR*, but the acts of hand-laying, prayer, anointing, and first greeting are no longer done in the assembly but in the *consignatorium* or in the baptistry itself. The first view the Faithful get of the neophytes is when they enter the church with the bishop and his clergy in procession to the singing of a litany. This is the introit of the Easter Mass. A certain formalizing and clericalizing of the reception event has begun to be evident.

Fourth, despite this kind of innovation in the later documents, they remain textually conservative, especially in the epiclesis prayer said by the bishop alone over the neophytes during the ceremony of their reception (now performed, as noted, in a place other than the church). This can be seen by comparing the texts of *AT* and *Gel*:

Apostolic Tradition	*Gelasian Sacramentary*
O Lord God,	Almighty God, Father of our Lord Jesus Christ,
who didst count these worthy of deserving the forgiveness of sins by the laver of regeneration,	who hast made thy servants to be regenerated of water and the Holy Spirit, and hast given them remission of all their sins,
make them worthy to be filled with thy Holy Spirit	do thou, Lord pour upon them thy Holy Spirit, the Paraclete,
and send upon them thy grace, that they may serve thee according to thy will;	and give them the spirit of wisdom and understanding, the spirit of counsel and might, the spirit of knowledge and godliness, and fill them with the spirit of fear of God,
to thee is the glory, to the Father and to the Son with the Holy Ghost in the holy Church, both now and ever . . .	in the name of our Lord Jesus Christ, with whom thou livest and reignest ever God, with the Holy Spirit, throughout all ages . . . [65]

The sequence is identical: only rhetorical rephrasing and some expansion from John 3.5 and Isaiah 11.2f has occurred in the later text.

Fifth, the catechumens are people of all ages, including children (who in *AT* are to be baptized first).[66] The initiatory pattern in both sets of documents is the way any and all are to be brought to baptism, no matter what their age. All are newborn ones—

neophytes, *infantes*. But inferences in the rubrics of *Gel* and *OR* make it clear that by the sixth to eighth centuries the subjects of initiation are in fact largely small children or babies. In *OR*, for example, the "infants" are carried (*deportantur*) before the bishop to receive their baptismal garments and to be "confirmed": they must also be kept from feeding at the breast (*ablactantur*) before they are given their first holy communion.[67] This, taken together with the fact that *OR* moved the time for the scrutinies from the third, fourth, and fifth lenten Sundays to weekdays, suggests that the old Christian catechumenate had become populated largely by very young children—so much so that their formal examination by the whole church met for Sunday worship was deemed unnecessary. It also implies that the multiform catechesis of Hippolytus and the early fathers had shrunk to the formal liturgical "catechizing" of the three scrutinies during lenten weekdays. Before long this same pastoral situation led to the demise of the old interogatory form for administering baptism still witnessed in *Gel*: the *Ordo Romanus XXVIII* of the ninth century says that, after having asked the old questions concerning belief of the parents in the Trinity, the bishop then takes the infant *de parentibus* and immerses it with a declaratory formula, *Baptizo te, in nomine patris . . . et filii . . . et spiritus sancti*.[68] And while in conservative Rome as late as the twelfth century the pope himself, wearing hip boots, descended into the great pool of the Lateran baptistry to baptize a symbolic number of children,[69] already in late ninth century France the very presence of bishops at the full rites of paschal initiation was becoming sporadic.[70]

Many churches of the west which followed their own liturgical traditions seem originally to have known no consignation with hand-laying and a second anointing with chrism. They came to accept Roman practice reluctantly only under pressure from the Carolingian state. When they finally did so, the consignation and anointing were performed either after communion at the baptismal mass, or in the same place *but a week later*, on the octave day of Easter. Northern theologians subsequently offered theoretical justification for what had already become a pastoral and liturgical fact when they explained the now separated invocation of the Spirit, hand-laying, and second anointing with chrism as an *increase* in initial baptismal grace.[71] The old Roman *consignatio* had been separated from its original baptismal context to float free, generating a theology to justify it apart from baptism. As Nathan Mitchell observes, "by the early ninth century we are well on the road to 'confirmation,' to a split in the ensemble of initiation rites, and to a style of theology that will legitimate them both. As a result, to write the story of the dissolution of Christian initiation is to write about the emergence of episcopal confirmation as a rite separated from baptism."[72]

The separation of the old Roman consignation from baptism—first by the intervening baptismal Mass, then by Easter week, and later by years as became the case within some three centuries—should be called what it is. It is a dissolution, not a development. It is "Roman" only to the extent that the Roman tradition settled for it in lieu of being able to get anything better by way of observance out of the other western churches undergoing a romanization of their polities at the time. The dissolution was thus originally a compromise whose legitimacy was established theologically only during the high scholastic period, and then by appeals to allegorical exegesis of the Old Testament or to spurious documents forged in the ninth century. Theologians of medieval European Catholicism did not cause the separation: they only legitimated what they inherited.[73] And the legitimation was such that, when coupled with the sort of practice that ensued by the sixteenth century, confirmation as a separate sacrament instituted by Jesus Christ could easily be called into question by theological and biblical scholars of the Reform.[74]

In reacting to the objections of the Reformers, the Council of Trent (1545–1563) canonized late medieval theology and practice regarding baptismal initiation for the Roman Catholic Church until the Second Vatican Council undertook its reforms shortly after the middle of this century.[75] Only one major development intervened during this period that touched initiatory polity, and its effect was to modify Roman initiatory sequence profoundly. In 1905 Pius X decreed that the Faithful were to be encouraged to receive holy communion with much greater frequency than had been the case since at least the ninth century, particularly on Sundays and feasts but even daily where possible. Five years later he lowered the age for receiving first communion from adolescence to the dawn of the use of reason in early childhood. This produced among many clergy and people on the parish level much concern over whether children of such age could learn enough catechism to know what communion was about—a concern which often became heated and led to widespread ignoring of the papal decree.[76] Yet it is notable that the concern expressed centered on matters of religious education and reverence for the blessed sacrament, not on the further isolation of confirmation in adolescence from baptism in infancy by inserting first communion between the two in early childhood. The shift of first communion from after confirmation (usually administered at this period in late childhood or early adolescence) not only placed the sacrament of penance prior to and preparatory for the eucharist in early childhood; it also left confirmation bereft of its psychological consummation in the experience of first communion, into which it had customarily admitted one.[77]

Thus only slightly more than a generation prior to the Second Vatican Council the Roman Rite had come to a polity of sacramental initiation which no longer recognized the *baptism-seal-eucharist* sequence of Hippolytus, nor the *baptism-consignation/confirmation-eucharist* pattern of the medieval and Counter-Reformation Church, but a wholly new procedure: *baptism-penance-communion-confirmation*. The catechumenate in preparation for baptism had ceased to exist; catechesis had been separated from the liturgy and deritualized; and what had once been a single initiatory process consummated in two paschal phases (baptism/consignation and eucharist) had now become four sacraments loosely based on personality development in preadolescent individuals and knit together by religious education and therapy programs to serve them.

NOTES

1. This principle was first enunciated in 1927 by Anton Baumstark, *Comparative Liturgy*, trans. F. L. Cross (A. R. Mowbray, London [3]1958) 27.

2. J.-P. Audet, *La didache. Instructions des Apôtres* (Librarie Lecoffre, Paris 1958) 187-210.

3. Even the two-day weekly fasts are Jewish, but chapter 8 specifies that Christians fast on Wednesdays and Fridays rather than on Mondays and Thursdays "with the hypocrites." The same chapter bases the "prayer" of Christians on the petitions of the Our Father, much as the "prayer" of the Jews was the eighteen petitions of *Shemoneh Esre* or *Tefilla*. See D. Hegegård, *Seder R. Amram Gaon* (Lindstedts Universitetsbokhandel, Lund 1951) 70f.

4. *Letter to the Smyrnaeans* 8:2. See Lampe 104-105.

5. See Sebastian Brock, "Studies in the Early History of the Syrian Orthodox Baptismal Liturgy," *Journal of Theological Studies* 23 (1972) 16-64; "The Syrian Baptismal Ordines," *Studia Liturgica* 12:4 (1978) 177-183; and Gabriele Winkler, "The Original Meaning of the Prebaptismal Anointing and Its Implications," *Worship* 52 (1978) 24-45. For the baptismal chapters of the *Acts of Thomas*, see E. C. Whitaker, *Documents of the Baptismal Liturgy* (SPCK, London 1960) 10-13; for that of the *Didascalia Apostolorum*, see Whitaker 9-10. The earliest extant texts of the *Armenian Ordo* are edited by Winkler, *Das armenische Initiationsrituale. Entwicklungsgeschichtliche und liturgievergleichende Untersuchung der Quellen des 3. bis 10. Jahrhunderts* (Oriental Institute, Rome 1979). Some of the *Ordo* is translated in Whitaker 52-59.

6. *Acts of Thomas*, chapters 27 and 132 (Whitaker 10-11 and 12).

7. *Acts of Thomas*, chapters 121 and 157 (Whitaker 11-12 and 12-13). Also *Didascalia Apostolorum*, chapter 16 (Whitaker 10).

8. *Apostolic Constitutions* 3:16-17; 7:22 and 44 (c. 380) (Whitaker 27-28, 31).

9. Thus Winkler, art. cit. 27.

10. Whitaker 11.

11. Whitaker 12, modified by Winkler, art. cit. 30.

12. Thus Winkler, ibid. 37. Compare this with Gregory Dix's less careful resumé, *The Shape of the Liturgy* (Dacre Press, London 1945) 260f.

13. An example of such a general prayer may be seen in the first letter of Clement of Rome to the church at Corinth (c. 95), chapters 59-61, in *The Apostolic Fathers*, vol. 1, ed. Kirsopp Lake in the Loeb Classical Library series (G. P. Putnam, New York 1919) 111-117.

14. Whitaker 2.

15. Lampe 110.

16. *Tertullian's Homily on Baptism*, ed. Ernest Evans (SPCK, London 1964) 5, henceforth cited as Evans. The work is not really a "homily" but the earliest theological treatise on baptism to have survived.

17. Evans 5-7.

18. *Apostolic Tradition* 16-20 (Whitaker 3-4); *On Baptism* 20 (Evans 41-43; Whitaker 7, quotes excerpts).

19. *Apostolic Tradition* 21 (Whitaker 4-5); *On Baptism* 4 (Evans 9-11, Whitaker 8).

20. *Apostolic Tradition* 21 (Whitaker 6); *On Baptism* 7 (Evans 17, Whitaker 8-9).

21. *Apostolic Tradition* 21-22 (Whitaker 6); *On Baptism* 8 (Evans 17-18, Whitaker 9).

22. *Apostolic Tradition* 23 (Whitaker 7); Tertullian in *De Corona* 3 (Whitaker 9).

23. E.g., Cyril of Jerusalem (c. 350–386), *Mystagogical Catecheses* 2 (Whitaker 25-26); Ambrose of Milan (c. 374–397), *Concerning the Sacraments* 3 (Whitaker 120).

24. See, for example, Tertullian's admonition to the newly baptized along these lines in Evans 43.

25. See Peter Brown, *The World of Late Antiquity* (Thames and Hudson, London 1971) 98.

26. In *Didache* 7 (Whitaker 1) the requirement of fasting for the baptized and the baptizer, and its recommendation to others who are able, signals this. Also in the *Acts of Thomas* 27 (Whitaker 11) baptismal remission of sins and its "purification of reins and hearts" is mentioned: in chapter 157 (Whitaker 13) it cleanses from former works.

27. *On Baptism* 7-8 (Evans 17-19, Whitaker 8-9). In *Apostolic Tradition* 22 (Whitaker 6) the newly baptized are prayed for to be filled with the Holy Spirit in the holy Church. Serving a cup of milk and honey to the neophytes at their first communion symbolized both their having entered the promised land and their newborn status as *infantes*: see chapter 23 (Whitaker 7).

28. Latin in *Inscriptiones Latinae Christianae Veteres*, ed. E. Diehl (Weidmann, Berlin 1925) vol. 1, 289.

29. Tertullian says that this anointing is "unto the priesthood" in *On Baptism* 7 (Evans 17, Whitaker 8-9): Hippolytus says it is "in the Name of Jesus Christ" in *Apostolic Tradition* 21 (Whitaker 6).

30. See *Apostolic Constitutions* 3:16 and 7:44 (Whitaker 27 and 31). Also the later *Barberini Euchologion*, the earliest (c. 790) full text of the liturgy of Constantinople (Whitaker 73).

31. Ambrose (+397), *Concerning the Sacraments* 3 (Whitaker 120-121) mentions a "spiritual seal" which ends the rite of reception.

32. See the earliest surviving complete Roman liturgical texts in the *Gelasian Sacramentary* of the eighth century in Whitaker 178, and the ceremonial descriptions correlative with them of the *Ordo Romanus XI* in Whitaker 193-194.

33. For *Bobbio*, see Whitaker 202; *Stowe*, Whitaker 210. Caution must be used when generalizing about later Latin texts, Roman or otherwise, since with few exceptions they do not report the given liturgy in its original state but mixed with other influences.

34. *Concerning the Sacraments* 3 (Whitaker 120-121); *Concerning the Mysteries* 29-42 (Whitaker 122-123).

35. The gesture may derive from the scene in Acts 8.14-17, in which Peter and John lay their hands upon the Samaritans baptized by Philip, thus making available the Spirit of the pentecostal church of Jerusalem by extending its communion to them. See Beasley-Murray 116-125.

36. E.g., J. M. Hanssens, *La Liturgie d'Hippolyte* (Oriental Institute, Rome 1959).

37. Thus Lampe xvii-xviii.

38. The *Gelasian Sacramentary* in its earliest extant form is found in a gallicanized version of the eighth century in the Vatican manuscript *Reginensis 316*. See A. Chavasse, *Le Sacramentaire Gélasien: Sacramentaire presbytéral en usage dans les titres romaines au VIIe siècle* (Bibliotheque de Théologie 4:

Histoire de Théologie 1, Tournai 1958); *Liber Sacramentorum Romanae Aeclesiae Ordinis Anni Circuli*, ed. Cunibert Mohlberg (Casa Editrice Herder, Rome 1968); Bernard Moreton, *The Eighth-Century Gelasian Sacramentary* (Oxford University Press, Oxford 1976). The Roman core of the *Gelasian* is some three centuries older, as is the *Ordo*. See Whitaker 156-186 for the initiatory section of the *Gelasian*, and 186-194 for *Ordo Romanus XI*. Hippolytan elements are also evident in the letter of John the Deacon to the Roman nobleman Senarius, c. 500 (Whitaker 144-148).

39. Neunheuser 164-165. The classic study of the relationship of the baptismal elements in *Gelasian* with those of *Ordo XI* remains Michel Andrieu's essay, "L'ordo XI et les sacramentaires romaines," in his monumental *Les Ordines Romani du Haute Moyen Age* (Spicilegium Sacrum Louvaniense, Louvain 1948) vol. 2, 380-408; see also his essay on Roman baptism, ibid. 409-413, and his critical text of the *Ordo*, 417-447.

40. Thus Tertullian, *On Baptism* 19 (Evans 41, Whitaker 7).

41. *AT* 16 (Whitaker 3).

42. *Gel* 71 (Whitaker 182). *OR* contains no rite of enrollment in the catechumenate, beginning only with the first scrutiny, in the third week of Lent, of those senior catechumens chosen for baptism at the following Easter.

43. *AT* 16-19 (Whitaker 3).

44. For a resumé of this, see Robert Grant's "Development of the Christian Catechumenate," in *Made, Not Born* 32-49.

45. *AT* 20 (Whitaker 4).

46. See Michel Dujarier, "Sponsorship," in *Adult Baptism and the Catechumenate*, ed. Johannes Wagner, Concilium Series 22 (Paulist Press, New York 1967) 45-50.

47. Pope Siricius, in a letter to Himerius of Tarragona dated 385, notes that the election of those to be baptized at Easter took place forty days before: see Andrieu, loc. cit. 382.

48. *OR* shifts these Sunday events to weekdays, a sure sign of the weakening of the discipline of the catechumenate during and after the seventh century.

49. Whitaker 145.

50. See Roger Béraudy, "Scrutinies and Exorcisms," in *Adult Baptism and the Catechumenate* 57-61; Balthasar Fischer, "Baptismal Exorcism in the Catholic Baptismal Rites after Vatican II," *Studia Liturgica* 10:1 (1974) 48-55.

51. *Gel* XXXIV-XXXVI (Whitaker 162-169); *OR* 1-75 (Whitaker 186-191). For symbolic reasons *OR* counts the scrutinies as seven, but the threefold number in *Gel* is the more original.

52. *Gel* XLII (Whitaker 173); *OR* 82-88 (Whitaker 192-193).

53. *AT* 20 (Whitaker 4).

54. *OR* 89 (Whitaker 193). So too *Gel* XLII, not included in Whitaker: see Mohlberg ed. 68-70. The first three lessons are from Genesis (creation, Noah and the flood, and Abraham), two are from Exodus, two from Isaiah, and one each from Ezekiel, Deuteronomy, and Daniel. The eleventh "lesson" is the singing of Psalm 42 ("As the deer thirsts for flowing streams . . . "), whose prayer following interprets its contents as a type of baptism. *Gel* XLIII (Whitaker 174-176).

55. *Gel* XLIV (Whitaker 176-178).

56. Nils Dahl thinks that the consecration of the water may be rooted in the first blessing prayer, or *berakah*, prescribed in rabbinic lore for a Jew who takes a ritual bath; also, the prohibition of alien objects seems to recall the *tebilah* requirement of "no separation" (*hasisah*) between the one immersed and the water. "The Origin of Baptism," in *Interpretationes ad Vetus Testamentum pertinentes S. Mowinckel* (Forlaget Land og Kirke, Oslo 1955) 46.

57. A Greek-speaking candidate would have heard this statement, which Hippolytus originally set down in Greek,

". . . in the Name of Jesus the Anointed One." The formula is clearly christic and messianic rather than pentecostal and pneumatic.

58. *AT* 20 (Whitaker 4-6).

59. Whitaker 178. So too *OR* 97 (Whitaker 193).

60. The text of the prayer is in *Gel* (Whitaker 178), but the term "confirm" nowhere appears. *OR* 100 is clear that the bishop "confirms" them with this prayer (*confirmans eos cum invocatione septiformis gratiae spiritus sancti*), which is an epiclesis.

61. *Gel*, ibid.; *OR* 98-103 (Whitaker 193-194).

62. *AT* 22 (Whitaker 6-7). The kiss of peace is not mentioned in *Gel* or *OR* because by their time the Roman liturgy had moved it from the end of the prayer of the faithful, just before the eucharist began, to its present location just before communion.

63. Thus the Council of Carthage (397), canon 5: "It was agreed that no sacrament should be given to catechumens, even during the most solemn Paschal season, except the usual salt: for if the faithful make no change in the sacrament during that season, it should not be changed for catechumens" (Whitaker 212).

64. See canon 24 of the same council (Whitaker 212) and the letter to Senarius of John the Deacon quoted above on pp. 59-60 (Whitaker 147-148).

65. *AT* 22 (Whitaker 6); *Gel* XLIV (Whitaker 178).

66. *AT* 21 (Whitaker 5).

67. *OR* 99-103 (Whitaker 193-194). This tendency is complete by the twelfth and thirteenth centuries, when liturgical manuscripts entitle the invocation of the Spirit upon the newly baptized variously as *ordo ad consignandos pueros, ad confirmandos infantes*, and *confirmatio puerorum*. See Nathan Mitchell, "Dissolution of the Rite of Christian Initiation," in *Made, Not Born* 61-62.

68. Andrieu, vol. 3, 407. This also signals the final de-

ritualization of catechesis in the dropping of the lenten scrutinies altogether.

69. [*Pontifex*] *exuit se de pallio et planeta, et induit bracalia cerata, et revertitur ad fontes et baptizet tres parvulos*. Quoted from Mabillon's *Ordo* XII, in Wolfred Nelson Cote, *The Archaeology of Baptism* (Yates and Alexander, London 1876) 168.

70. Thus *Ordo Romanus XV: Baptizati autem infantes*, si ad praesens episcopum habere, *confirmari cum crisma debent. Quod si ipsa die* minime episcopum inveniri potuerint, *in quantum celerius possunt invenire, hoc sine dilatione ficiant*. Andrieu, vol. 3, 119. The implication here is that even *finding* a bishop who would preside at baptism, much less confirm, was a problem in the non-Roman churches of the north.

71. See N. Mitchell 55-56.

72. Ibid. 56. See J. D. C. Fisher, *Christian Initiation. Baptism in the Medieval West* (SPCK, London 1965).

73. See N. Mitchell 64-70 for an excellent review of Aquinas' methodology and pneumatically sophisticated theology of confirmation. Alexander Schmemann, in *Of Water and the Spirit* (St. Vladimir's Seminary Press, New York 1974) 76-77, is wrong when he implies that scholastic theories on grace caused confirmation to be separated from baptism in the west. This had already occurred prior to the scholastic period.

74. See J. D. C. Fisher, *Christian Initiation. The Reformation Period* (SPCK, London 1970); Leonel L. Mitchell, "Christian Initiation: The Reformation Period," in *Made, Not Born* 83-98.

75. Trent's position on initiation was synthesized liturgically in the *Rituale Romanum* (1614) and the *Pontificale Romanum (1595)*, books which for the first time made exclusive use of their contents by all western churches in communion with Rome a matter of law.

76. One American pastor as late as 1929 wrote: "I almost had to defend myself with a gun because I introduced the custom of taking the little ones to First Communion at the

age set down in the decree of Pius X." See Paul B. Marx, *Virgil Michel and the Liturgical Movement* (The Liturgical Press, Collegeville, Minnesota 1957) 95.

77. When the same shift of communion prior to confirmation was proposed in the Church of England in the early 1940s, the conservative bishop of Oxford, K. E. Kirk, labeled it "modernist" and "dangerous." See Dale Moody, *Baptism: Foundations for Christian Unity* (Westminster Press, Philadelphia 1967) 169-172.

The Reforms

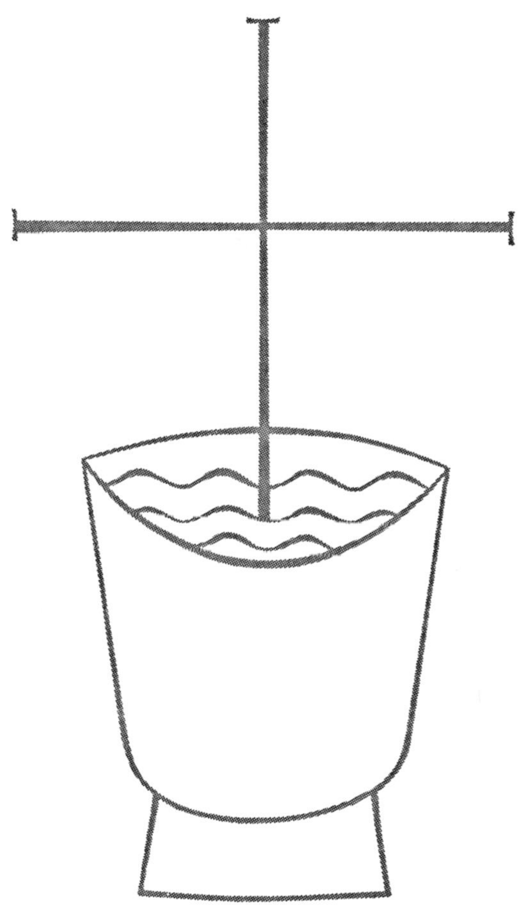

Chapter Three

The Reforms of the Second Vatican Council: The Context

The state of initiatory practice in the Roman Rite during the four decades preceding the Second Vatican Council was in a degree of confusion intensified if not wholly induced by unilateral papal action. For example, one thing the lowering of the age at which first communion could be given did was to telescope definitively the whole of sacramental initiation into the years of earliest childhood, loading no less than three sacraments (penance, eucharistic communion, and confirmation), together with instructional preparation for each, into these years. Not only did this enhance the necessity of the parochial elementary school, especially in the United States, but three further things resulted.

First, confirmation and holy communion (in whatever sequence they were observed) were brought into closer chronological proximity to baptism in infancy than had been the case for centuries. This meant, secondly, that the medieval and Counter-Reformation emphasis on confirmation—and on the eucharist also, if only by implication and to a lesser extent—as the sacrament of "maturity" was at least partially undercut.

These first two results made a rethinking of confirmation inevitable because change in eucharistic practice necessitated modification in the customary ways confirmation was to be explained if it was to be administered at so early an age.[1] Confirmation's new proximity to baptism in infancy meant furthermore that baptism would unavoidably exercise a greater influence on the perception of confirmation than it had for centuries. From another angle, if in recasting the theory of confirmation due to a change in its practice one came to see confirmation as being thus-and-so, then what was baptism? While not a new question (the scholastics had wrestled with it extensively in their attempts to legitimate confirmation as a sacrament separate from baptism seven centuries earlier), its restatement was given added urgency by the pastoral situation of the Church in an age of upheavals stemming from the social, political, industrial, and technological revolutions of the late eighteenth through the twentieth centuries. The main sacramental concern in such an era would have less to do with the nature of confirmation in itself than with who a Christian is in such a world, and with how he or she comes to be one. This signaled that the debate would be controlled ultimately by the theory and practice of baptism more than by any other factor.

But the third result of confirmation's having migrated into early childhood had the power to derail the debate, distracting the debaters by a matter of pastoral urgency. The migration left a large sacramental vacuum in the years of adolescence. In earlier centuries, adolescence had been a period of the greatest social brevity, if it could be said to have existed at all: a young person went straight from childhood into the responsibilities of adulthood with scarcely any pause sanctioned by society.[2] With the coming of the need for universal literacy caused by the invention of printing in the fifteenth century, compounded by technology's information explosion and the need for complex skills to serve its sophisticated apparatus, increasingly extended schooling pushed the period of true childhood farther back toward birth and the time of adult majority forward onto the verge of middle age. The intervening period, stretching finally from primary schooling to the attainment of a graduate degree in one's late twenties or early thirties, gradually became a time of extended adolescence in which the liberties of being a child and the restrictions of being a responsible adult met, tangled, and produced individuals often consumed by anxiety and maimed by the lack of a strong sense of social and personal identity. The churches no less than the secular societies in which they existed thus found themselves populated increasingly by deracinated young people prepared to submit themselves to whatever ideology might offer them a sense of identity strong enough to overwhelm their own anxiety and lack of purpose or direction.

The pastoral crisis this situation still presents is of such vast proportions that debate about it transcends the concerns of a few scholars and persons with ecclesiastical tastes. But the debate is on no small matter, nor is it confined to academe or sacristies. It is a question to be faced by all those who care about the survival of that creative force, the Church of Jesus Christ, which fostered the rise of western culture. The whole question has been complicated by the fact that serious consideration has been given to putting confirmation as the sacrament of maturity back into adolescence (somewhere, it seems, between thirteen and thirty), and that doing so would really and almost by itself produce the sort of person the modern Church needs to survive and fulfill its mission. As well-intentioned as this attempt was— it used confirmation so conceived as the special basis for manifestations such as the German Catholic *Jugendverein* and French and American Catholic Social Action movements in the 1930s—and as sophisticated as some of its theory became,[3] the centering of so much concern on this singular sacramental event could compete neither with the massive initiatory structure of modern educational systems nor with the monstrous totalitarian appeals represented in communist and fascist state socialism.

One senses that the situation to which these secular competitors responded earlier has since changed only to the extent that its point of focus has shifted somewhat—away from external, objective, and social dimensions toward the internal, subjective, and personal. Overcoming one's anxiety and attaining a sense of one's Christian identity is now sought less by appeal to the areas of politics and social change than by involvement in a variety of therapies.[4] Totalitarianism finds it less effective to shoot dissenters than to confine them in psychiatric institutions: they are not politically wrong so much as psychologically deranged and thus in need of therapy. Christians reproduce this trend by seeing the sacraments as educationally therapeutic occasions. Confirmation, it has been suggested, should perhaps evolve into a repeatable rite which could respond to psychic and social changes in one's maturing commitment to Jesus Christ. Or the sacrament might be used (as one American diocesan official put it in 1972) as "a real gesture for people after they are married, perhaps when they have a child ready for baptism or for school or for first communion."[5] In the first suggestion, confirmation becomes a sacrament of spiritual sensitivity; in the second, a hospitable gesture to Christian parents not unlike the medieval churching of mothers after childbirth.

The debate over initiatory practice occasioned by the modern pastoral situation and precipitated by the migration of penance, eucharist, and confirmation into the years of early childhood became largely preoccupied with rethinking confirmation in ways that might legitimate its return to a later age-period where some affirmation of one's faith seemed badly needed. In retrospect one cannot help concluding that this rethinking resulted in proposed solutions that smack of clericalism and a narrow, unhealthy sort of ritualism, however well intentioned. For a while confirmation was confidently spoken of as the laity's "ordination" to the "official" lay apostolate.[6] Since the Council the trend has continued: some charismatics have begun to suggest that confirmation be seen as that baptism in the Spirit which marks off, in rather gnostic and elitist fashion, the true follower of Christ from his or her merely baptized, and thus less gifted, colleagues.

The thrust of all these suggestions was to nudge confirmation back toward the years of adolescence or early adulthood. So frequent were these suggestions that they generated a presumption that came largely to be accepted as a first principle of debate and pastoral reform during the middle decades of this century. Thus the migration of confirmation into early childhood after 1910 was only sporadic and relatively shortlived:[7] in German and English-speaking countries especially, confirmation tended to go back into the years of adolescence where it now stood alone, no longer the overture to first communion as its emotionally laden outcome. Being no longer buttressed either by baptism immediately preceding it or by first communion after, confirmation was now a great deal more free to assume whatever variety of interpretations might seem pastorally or ideologically appropriate. It became once again a rite seeking a rationale.

Not only did this mean that confirmation began to take precedence in the mounting discussion on initiatory polity in Roman Catholic circles; it also began to overshadow baptism and thus distract the discussion. The reemergence of confirmation in adolescence or early adulthood as the sacrament peculiar to one's mature assumption of public responsibilities in Church and society had the effect of reenforcing the presumption that baptism was the sacrament peculiar to birth and infancy. In that position, baptism was the wholly necessary exorcism of original sin and the occasion of the infant's being lent sufficient faith by the Church, through the good offices of godparents and parents, to see it through to the critical stage when, as an individual on the verge of "maturity," that faith could be appropriated by the former infant in his or her own right—namely, in confirmation. Liturgical practice validated this perception on the people's part. Baptism was done by a simple priest or even layperson as soon after birth as feasible, in the parish church or hospital, privately and apart from regular community worship with only family and a few friends present.[8] Confirmation, however, was a high point of the parish year, presided over by the bishop at a major event of public worship and prepared for weeks or months in advance by intensive instruction of the recipients. Confirmation could not but seem at least on a par with baptism. In such a context, further ideological emphasis on confirmation as the sacrament of Christian maturity *par excellence* made it a baptismal surrogate in practice if not in theory.

BAPTISMAL DEBATES: 1937–1964

In such a situation, it began to appear that fresh work on baptism itself was urgently in order. For it began to occur to Christian thinkers of diverse confessional backgrounds that modern problems of Christian identity, both individual and ecclesial, had much to do with initiatory polity, and the core of that polity was baptism rather than confirmation in its various medieval and Reformation forms.

The work was begun in continental Reformed Churches with an attack on infant baptism, mounted less on biblical than personalist-philosophical grounds, by Emil Brunner in 1937.[9] This elicited agreement by Karl Barth in 1943 that baptism, being essentially an act of faith requiring cognition, lay beyond infant capacity.[10] The same tack was taken up and expanded into an attack on the sacramentality of baptism itself by his son, Markus Barth, in 1951.[11] The scale of this attack by three of Europe's best known Protestant scholars evoked a defense of infant baptism and, at least to some extent, its sacramental nature and liturgical modality by other Reformed theologians such as F.-J. Leenhardt, P. C. Marcel, and Oscar Cullmann.[12] Lutherans also joined the debate, early among them Joachim Jeremias supporting the Cullmann group,[13] and Kurt Aland in opposition.[14]

Stirrings of the debate can be detected in the Church of England as early as 1937, but after the Second World War the issues rapidly shifted from infant baptism to the meaning of confirmation and its relation to baptism as a result of the liturgical research of Gregory Dix. Adopting a position on the matter that had already been advanced by A. J. Mason in 1891, Dix maintained that baptism and confirmation had been separate entities from the very beginning, and that water baptism was both preparatory for and incomplete without the sealing with the Holy Spirit in confirmation.[15] This position, which was sometimes called the "Mason-Dix Line," evoked a storm of controversy and a considerable literature, the most representative work in opposition being that of G. W. H. Lampe, who criticized not only Dix but his major sources, Tertullian and Hippolytus, for separating water baptism from Spirit baptism: Lampe sees this as gnostic in origin and Pelagian in tendency.[16] This strong critique of the Mason-Dix position prompted L. S. Thornton to come to Dix's aid with a thorough if somewhat eccentric restatement of the medieval scholastic legitimation of confirmation updated in modern terms.[17]

But it would be misleading to suggest that the debates, whether on the continent or in England, were only abstract disagreements among scholars over infant baptism and confirmation. The issues were joined over the parlous state of the churches that was laid bare by the advent of European fascism and by the chaos wrought upon the churches by the Second World War. On the continent the involvement of Reformed and, especially, Lutheran Churches with the secular state raised questions about Christian identity and witness as effects of baptism. In England the pastoral situation was somewhat different, but pastoral urgency about the gradual dechristianization of the masses due, as it seemed to many, to the formalism of Established Church practice was no less real. Here particularly a sense of baptism's having shrunk to little more than getting an infant "done" for social reasons was pastorally worrisome. The concern, which began to be addressed in a series of meetings and reports of various official organizations in the Established Church from 1936, is the context within which the Dix-Lampe-Thornton debate took place. It quickly defined the problem in England as being that of "indiscriminate baptism" mandated by laws dating from a time when Christendom—that era when Church and State were conceived of as being distinct yet correlative functions of each other—had been alive and well. Unable or unwilling to postpone baptism, some British clergy suggested that devotional preparation for first communion during late childhood, even prior to confirmation in middle or late adolescence, might provide some degree of Christian nurture before the individual's personality had set and he or she was lost to the faith. Others suggested moving to a policy of "believers baptism," restoring the ancient catechumenate with baptism occurring at the usual time confirmation had come to be administered. Others yet urged adoption of the practice observed in Orthodox Churches, in which the infant is baptized, confirmed, and given first communion.[18]

Roman Catholicism was left untouched neither by the pastoral situation nor the debates on baptism spawned in continental Prostestant circles and in the Church of England. But to a more pronounced degree than was usual in these churches, Roman Catholic discussion of baptism was affected by two factors that gave a distinctiveness to its theory and practice, especially during the late 1940s and 1950s.

For one thing, Roman Catholics could not simply jettison an Augustinianism that ran through the medieval scholasticism to which their Church had given normative theological value. This meant that whenever the baptismal core of the discussion and possible reform were touched, the matter of baptism's absolute necessity and its immediate (*quamprimum*) administration to infants came quickly to the fore. In turn, the question of the meaning of original sin had to be broached as the setting within which conventional Catholic theory and practice could be reviewed. The ensuing debate revealed that some liberalization had taken place among Catholic scholars since Herman Schells' *Katholische Dogmatik*, which suggested in 1893 that unbaptized infants might attain to some state more exalted even than limbo, had been put on the Index of Forbidden Books.[19] In general these scholars were beginning to view original sin as the objective existential milieu that gives rise to acts of sin by which an individual incurs personal guilt, thus earning condemnation while at the same time contributing to and supporting the existential condition which provides a viable milieu for sin. In this view one is not born into a state of innocence, but neither is one guilty of sin before God by the fact of being born *per se*. Born into a condition of existential sinfulness, the infant cannot but surely sin, thereby appropriating to itself that condition in a culpable manner. Born into the *servitus diaboli* (to use Augustine's own phrases against the Pelagians), and languishing *sub diaboli potestate*, the human being will ultimately become personally culpable as *servus diaboli* and *vasa eius* unless access to the wholly special resources of God's grace in Christ is provided.

Advances in patristic studies had enabled Catholic scholars to see this position as the one generally held by church fathers prior to the fourth century, when Augustine (354–430) was born. Two things compelled him to impute guilt to unbaptized infants. The first was the Pelagian position's denial of original sin, and its insistence that human beings can indeed attain salvation by their own efforts—a position that appeared to lay waste orthodox views of redemption in Christ and atomize Christian life into little more than a form of individualistic moral stoicism.

The second factor was that by Augustine's time the baptism of infants was settling in as the usual way one became a Christian. The liturgy by which *all* people, regardless of age, were baptized was one. As we have seen, it involved enrollment in the catechumenate; instructions with hand-layings, exorcisms, scrutinies, election, baptismal anointings, consignation (in the west), and the eucharist. Yet this grand liturgy, celebrated over a period of years for the adults in view of whom it originally evolved, had come to be telescoped into a swollen ritual act performed all at one time when it was brought to bear on infants.[20] Augustine based his arguments against Pelagius chiefly on the practice of infant baptism *with its exorcisms*. The devil is driven out even from newly born children, and this is done not metaphorically but literally.[21] Since these exorcisms were originally meant for adults, who had indeed incurred personal guilt by actual sins, their application to infants, who had not yet been guilty of actual sins, served to transfer the dimension of personal guilt into the notion of original sin. Thus a doctrine of original sin involving personal culpability for everyone did not produce change in liturgical practice: rather, change in liturgical practice concerning infant baptism produced the Augustinian concept of original sin as necessarily implying personal guilt. This in turn not only legitimated infant baptism theologically, but it increasingly put a premium upon its administration *quamprimum* after birth.

Another factor that gave a distinctiveness to Roman Catholic theory and practice concerning baptism in the decade prior to the summoning of the Second Vatican Council in 1959, and which in some ways touched off the new round of debates over infant baptism and original sin mentioned above, was the restoration of the paschal vigil by Pope Pius XII in 1951.[22] This event, a highwater mark of the modern liturgical movement which had produced no less than fifty-seven papal documents on the liturgy between 1903 and 1953,[23] brought back to the attention of theologians and injected forcibly into the popular consciousness the pre-Augustinian Roman liturgical formulas touching baptism in its paschal context.[24]

It would be difficult to overestimate the importance of this event, for it set in motion the train of strategic overhauls in Catholic baptismal practice mandated by the Second Vatican Council from 1960 through 1963 and accomplished in the new orders for baptism of children (1969), for confirmation (1971), and for initiation of adults (1972). In a period of twenty-one years from 1951 the Roman Catholic baptismal liturgy was gradually shorn of many later non-Roman elements and restored to its original context in the Church's public worship at the paschal summit of the Christian year. Not only did these developments in general restore to the very center of Church practice a set of powerful rites which *in themselves* owe little or nothing to the neo-Augustinianism of medieval scholastics, but as part of over three-quarters of a century of liturgical reform they bear witness to a far less atomized and more holistic view of sacramental worship in the Church's life.[25] Alois Stenzel, for example, notes:

"If it is true that there are not two ways to the God of grace (one by way of faith, the other by way of the sacraments), but only the one; if it is true that the sacrament is the inwardness of faith given corporeal expression in the visibility of the Church; if it is true that such a sacramental event is not merely an appended 'visible word,' but the Church's most profound self-realization—then the whole way of faith in the Church must be followed sacramentally. In other words, baptism as the sacrament of faith must be an event coextensive with the stages of the development of faith. And that is just what history shows it to be."[26]

In this view baptism could not be merely an exorcistic rite to cope with infant culpability until such time as confirmation would publicly manifest an adolescent's faith and incorporate him or her into full church life and rights.[27] Rather, baptism is the paradigm of how faith in Jesus Christ is to be lived. It is a pastoral-sacramental process of nurture that both stretches back prior to the water bath into catechesis, conversion, and initial evangelization, and extends after it into the living of a sacramental life of faith, prayer, good works, and asceticism. This restoration of baptism's sacramental scope as incorporation into Christ in his Church overflows the singular rite of the water bath even though it reaches its most intense point of focus there. Thus, "Catechumens who, moved by the Holy Spirit, seek with explicit intention to be incorporated into the Church are by that very intention joined to her," said the Second Vatican Council. "With love and solicitude Mother Church already embraces them as her own."[28] The sacramental reality of life in Christ is structured by rites, but it is neither contained nor exhausted by them: only the Church itself, the Spirit-quickened Body of Christ, is of such scope as to house such a life adequately. It is a life whose style is that of a holistic art rather than a series of separate quasi-mechanical events.

In retrospect one may sense that a greater ferment concerning baptism and its ramifications for theology and pastoral practice was afoot in preconciliar Roman Catholicism than was perhaps perceived at the time. The building of a critical mass—as evidenced in the acute pastoral crises brought to a new degree of intensity in the aftermath of the Second World War, in the baptismal debates being carried on in European churches and in England, and in the subtle shifts occasioned by the restoration of the paschal vigil—was pressing Roman Catholic thinkers to recast their accustomed approaches to baptism in a manner perhaps unequaled since Augustine's time. Nowhere is the pressure more clearly seen than in the French church shortly before and during the Council. Here struggles with postwar crises, combined with attempts to incorporate the results of research into baptism and the opportunities afforded by the restoration of the paschal vigil, produced a literature on Christian initiation that remains perhaps the richest in modern Roman Catholicism. Three examples must suffice.

Already in 1947, Ch.-V. Heris had emphasized the necessity of faith in baptism when dealing with the question of the salvation of unbaptized infants. Moody sums up his position:

"As usual in the Roman tradition no question is raised as to the guilt of infants in original sin, but the primacy of faith, as in Thomas Aquinas and Cardinal Cajetan, approaches a view of justification by faith not always stated so clearly even in the baptismal theology of Lutheranism. No plea is made for infant faith, for infants are passive in the regeneration of the spiritual life as they are in the generation of natural life. It is the act of faith of their parents within the faith of the church that is sufficient . . ."[29]

Heris was clearly struggling with the demands of faith unto salvation on the one hand, and the necessity of baptism for salvation on the other, as had Augustine fifteen hundred years earlier.

Six years later, basing himself on a statement of doctrinal principles issued by the French bishops in 1951, A. M. Roguet held that with the baptism of infants it is not the faith of parents or godparents but the faith of the Church which is operative in the sacrament. But for Roguet the problem is not infant baptism in itself that tends to block the vital relation between God's grace and personal faith. It is, rather, indiscriminate baptism that produces a pathological situation:

"One might ask oneself, as do many priests today in anguish, if such baptisms should be celebrated at all; if they are not doing more harm than good, by weighing down the Church with a multitude of Christians who are so only in name, and who do harm to the

Church by confirming unbelievers in their opinion that, far from being a living society, a leaven that should raise the world's mass, the Church is a worn-out institution, ineffective, unreal, surviving only by custom."[30]

While Roguet made no specific proposals for changes in practice, his criticism of indiscriminate baptism was heard, and it led in 1957 to experiments in the Latin Quarter of Paris with adult initiation as the norm. A brief catechumenate of lenten duration was introduced; instruction was centered on the water themes of creation, the flood, and the crossing of the Red Sea; immersion was the manner of baptism; confirmation followed as an increase in baptismal grace through the Holy Spirit; and the eucharist completed the initiatory sequence.[31]

The increasing concern evident in Roguet for moving toward an adult emphasis in initiatory practice was sustained in the work of A. G. Martimort, who often stressed adult baptism as the norm and immersion as the mode of administration that best does justice to the sacramental meaning of the rite. Yet he follows Heris and the Augustinian-scholastic tradition in the opinion that faith is lent to infants by Church and parents, emphasizing this as a striking manifestation of the complete gratuity of the gift of God. Further, he urges no delay in baptizing infants, observing that such a delay indicates the dechristianization of a country or an environment.[32]

In the French literature one may thus detect stresses not yet reconciled—increasing emphasis on the adult nature of baptismal *meaning* in a critical pastoral situation, combined with a continuation, indeed a reenforcement, of *quamprimum* baptismal *practice* still centering on infants. A trumpet had begun to sound, but uncertainly. While fertile suggestions were being cautiously made, and in some areas being tried out, they were not of such depth or vigor as to resist being overwhelmed by a certain collapse of church discipline and morale in France during the 1960s.[33] Thus from 1958 to 1968 the rate of baptisms to births in France generally declined by almost 1% a year. In Paris itself 75% of the infants born in 1958 were baptized, while only 56% were baptized ten years later—a decline of almost a quarter. Furthermore, Easter had slight effect on the number of baptisms in the city: from 1958 to 1972 almost 30% of baptisms were celebrated in the months of May and June, as against some 18% during March and April when Easter occurred (and by no means all of these would have been done at the vigil).[34] In a poll conducted in 1972, 49% of adults and over 70% of youths between the ages of fifteen and nineteen said they would prefer to have their children baptized not at birth but later. The choices ranged from a few months to a few years: over half the youth and almost 30% of the adults said they would simply leave the matter for the child to choose—an ominous statistic probably indicating religious indifference more than concern for theological meaning and sacramental integrity.[35]

The example of the French church provides no simple lessons that can be applied in other countries without considerable caution. Its problems, at least in degree and to some extent in their form, are peculiarly French. Its structure, involving an intellectual elite at marked distance from the ordinary Catholic, is not wholly matched in North America. The society within which it exists is stratified to an extent unknown in the United States. But it cannot be denied that it has led the way in recovering for Roman Catholicism generally a sense of the proportions its initiatory polity took in the premedieval period, and could or must take again. The resourcefulness and depth of French scholarship in the area of Christian initiation provided the richest reservoir of both theoretical and practical data available when the Second Vatican Council embarked on its program of liturgical reform after 1959.

NOTES

1. The old sequence of baptism-confirmation-eucharist remained legally presumed by the 1918 *Code of Canon Law* in its section on these sacraments; see canons 737-869.

2. Reflecting this earlier state, canon 1067 recognizes the age at which one may contract a valid marriage as fourteen for females and sixteen for males.

3. See, for example, the series of three articles by Virgil Michel, "Confirmation: Our Apathy," "Confirmation: Its Divine Powers," and "Confirmation: Call to Battle," in *Orate Fratres* 2 (1928) 167-171, 199-204, 234-239. Michel was one of the most prolific and influential writers in Catholic liturgy, education, and social theory during the depression years until his death in 1938. See Paul B. Marx, *Virgil Michel and the Liturgical Movement* (The Liturgical Press, Collegeville, Minnesota 1957), especially 191-194.

4. See Philip Rieff, *The Triumph of the Therapeutic: Uses of Faith after Freud* (Harper and Row, New York 1966).

5. Quoted in Aidan Kavanagh, "Initiation: Baptism and Confirmation," *Worship* 46 (1972) 273.

6. See, for example, Marx 193. Underlying this conception is the medieval view that confirmation *confers* the Holy Spirit in a mode or to a degree that goes beyond what baptism does, thus increasing and strengthening (*ad robur*) baptismal grace. See Nathan Mitchell, "Dissolution of the Rite of Christian Initiation," in *Made, Not Born* 55-56; also P.-T. Camelot, "La théologie de la Confirmation à la lumière des controverses recentes," *La Maison-Dieu* 54 (1958) 79-91, and "Sur la théologie de la confirmation," *Revue des Sciences Philosophiques et Théologiques* 38 (1954) 637-657. Camelot's views are abstracted in "Toward a

Theology of Confirmation," *Theology Digest* 7 (1959) 67-71. Also Max Thurian, *La Confirmation. Consécration des laïcs* (Delachaux & Niestlé, Neuchâtel 1957).

7. Except in Spanish-speaking countries, where the older custom of confirmation close to the age of baptism in infancy and prior to first communion (given only later) has never died out despite its apparent banning prior to the age of seven. Thus canon 788: *Licet sacramenti confirmationis administratio convenienter in Ecclesia Latina differatur ad septimum circiter aetatis annum, nihilominus etiam antea conferri potest . . .*

8. An admonition of the Holy Office in 1958, *Acta Apostolicae Sedis* 50 (1958) 114, insisted so strongly on the immediate (*quamprimum*) administration of baptism after birth (as in canon 770) that in some places fonts began to be installed in Catholic hospitals and baptisms of all infants born in them performed there rather than in the parents' parish church. Had the Second Vatican Council not been summoned the following year, it is possible that this development would have spread, lending to baptism— already centered on infancy as the de facto norm—a pronounced clinical character. Canon 746 had already authorized intrauterine baptism in cases of necessity.

9. *Wahrheit als Begegnung* (Zwingli-Verlag, Zurich 1938), published in English as *Truth as Encounter* (Westminster Press, Philadelphia 1964) in a revised edition. Brunner's position has changed over the years to one of cautious and highly qualified acceptance of infant baptism: see Dale Moody, *Baptism: Foundation for Christian Unity* (Westminster Press, Philadelphia 1967) 50-55, the fullest general review in English of the debates over initiation since the Second World War.

10. *The Teaching of the Church Regarding Baptism*, trans. E. A. Payne (SCM Press, London 1948); Moody 57-64.

11. *Die Taufe: ein Sacrament?* (Evangelischer Verlag, Zollikon-Zurich 1951); Moody 67-71.

12. F.-J. Leenhardt, *Le Baptême chrétien, son origine, sa signification* (Delachaux & Niestlé, Neuchâtel 1946); Moody 77-79. P. C. Marcel, *The Biblical Doctrine of Infant Baptism:*

Sacrament of the Covenant of Grace (1950), trans. P. E. Hughes (J. Clarke & Company, London 1953); Moody 79-85. Oscar Cullmann, *Baptism in the New Testament* (1948), trans. J. K. S. Reid (SCM Press, London 1950); Moody 87-89.

13. *Infant Baptism in the First Four Centuries* (1958), trans. D. Cairns (Westminster Press, Philadelphia 1962); Moody 127-142. Jeremias had published on the question since 1938.

14. *Did the Early Church Baptize Infants?* (1961), trans. G. R. Beasley-Murray (Westminster Press, Philadelphia 1963); Moody 142-160.

15. A. J. Mason, *The Relation of Confirmation to Baptism* (Longmans, Green & Co., London 1891); Gregory Dix, *The Theology of Confirmation in Relation to Baptism* (Dacre Press, London 1946).

16. *The Seal of the Spirit* (1951) 124-127; "Baptism and Confirmation in the Light of the Fathers," in *Becoming a Christian*, ed. B. Minchin (Faith Press, London 1954) 34f.

17. *Confirmation: Its Place in the Baptismal Mystery* (Dacre Press, London 1954).

18. Moody 160-190. For the various reforms advanced, see Moody 207-215.

19. Moody 14-32 samples various positions advanced in the 1940s and 1950s among Catholic theologians.

20. This fusion process has been unraveled by G. Kretschmar, "Die Geschichte des Taufgottesdienstes in der alten Kirche," in *Leitourgia. Handbuch des evangelischen Gottesdienstes* 5 (J. Stauda Verlag, Kassel 1970) 1-348.

21. Thus G. M. Lukken, *Original Sin in the Roman Liturgy. Research into the Theology of Original Sin in the Roman Sacramentaria and the Early Baptismal Liturgy* (E. J. Brill, Leiden 1973) 198-200.

22. Undertaken at the request of the bishops of Germany, France, and Austria in 1950, the new *Ordo Sabbati Sancti* was issued in February of 1951 for experimental use the following Easter. The *Ordo* was subsequently used,

studied, and modified through 1955, when the reform was extended to the whole liturgy of the Holy Week.

23. Ten by Pius X, four by Benedict XV, twelve by Pius XI, and thirty-one by Pius XII. See A. Bugnini, *Documenta Pontificia ad Instaurationem Liturgicam* (Editione Liturgiche, Rome 1953); Marx 72-105.

24. See H. Schmidt, *Hebdomada Sancta* (Herder, Rome 1957).

25. See L. Brinkhoff, "Chronicle of the Liturgical Movement," in *Liturgy in Development*, ed. Alting von Geusau (Sheed and Ward Stagbooks, London 1965) 40-67.

26. "Temporal and Supra-Temporal in the History of the Catechumenate and Baptism," in *Adult Baptism and the Catechumenate*, Concilium Series 22 (Paulist Press, New York 1967) 37.

27. See Anselme Robeyns, "Rights of the Baptized," *Theology Digest* 10 (1962) 106-112.

28. Dogmatic Constitution on the Church, *Lumen Gentium*, 14, in *The Documents of Vatican II*, ed. Walter M. Abbott (America Press, New York 1966) 32-33, henceforth cited as Abbott. Also the Decree on Missions, *Ad Gentes*, 13-14 (Abbott 599-601); Constitution on the Liturgy, *Sacrosanctum Concilium*, 64-68 (Abbott 159-160).

29. Moody 23. Ch.-V. Heris, "Le salut des enfants morts sans baptême," *La Maison-Dieu* 10 (1947) 86-105.

30. *Christ Acts Through Sacraments*, trans. by the Carisbrooke Dominicans (The Liturgical Press, Collegeville, Minnesota, 1954) 62.

31. The liturgical model was adapted, by way of the rite for adult baptism in the *Roman Pontifical*, from that found in the eighth-century Gelasian Sacramentary, researched by A. Chavasse in many essays beginning in the 1940s and culminating in his *Le Sacramentaire Gélasien: Sacramentaire presbytéral en usage dans les titres romaines au VIIe siècle* (1958). Chavasse's scholarly work on the baptismal liturgy of the Gelasian was popularized in Th. Maertens' helpful *Histoire et pastorale du rituel du catéchuménat et du Baptême* (Publica-

tions de Saint-André, Bruges 1962). See also A. M. Carré, *Baptized in Christ*, trans. S. W. Griffiths (The Liturgical Press, Collegeville, Minnesota, 1957); Moody 24-25. The same proposals had been made, as we have seen, ten years earlier in the Church of England. See Moody 184-188.

32. *The Signs of the New Covenant* (The Liturgical Press, Collegeville, Minnesota, 1963) 135-136. Moody 21 incorrectly identifies him as a Benedictine.

33. See, for example, the extended tract of L. Bouyer, *The Decomposition of Catholicism* (1968), trans. C. U. Quinn (Franciscan Herald Press, Chicago 1969).

34. See J. Potel, *Moins de baptêmes en France. Pourquoi?* (Les Editions du Cerf, Paris 1974) especially 15-24.

35. Potel 98-99.

Chapter Four

The Reforms of the Second Vatican Council: The Norm of Baptism

Despite the richness of French research into initiation during the decade or so that preceded the convening of the Second Vatican Council on October 11, 1962,[1] there had not been any galvanizing public debate over baptism in Roman Catholic circles equal to those between Karl Barth and Oscar Cullmann in continental Reformed Churches, or between Gregory Dix and G. W. H. Lampe in the Church of England. It might not be too much to say that Catholic sentiment centered more naturally, so far as looked-for conciliar reforms were concerned, on doing something about the Mass. Catholic research on eucharistic matters had been far more extensive and of longer duration than research on baptism, and dates back even prior to the Council of Trent in the sixteenth century. One finds it hard to escape the impression that preconciliar Catholics looked at the most for a few tactical reforms in the Mass—such as some vernacular being allowed, a certain simplification of the rubrics, a restoration of the chalice to the laity under certain conditions, permission for concelebration at times, and perhaps the allowance for Mass to be celebrated facing the people. Even these expectations seemed remote in 1959, and advocacy of them was enough to render suspect even a saintly and distinguished clergyman such as Hans Ansgar Reinhold on the part of many American bishops and clergy until well after the Council had ended.[2]

Thus the Council's treatment of the reform of the Mass in its *Constitution on the Sacred Liturgy* (1963) is relatively extensive and detailed.[3] It was the first set of reforms to be undertaken by the postconciliar commission charged with the execution of the Council's wishes as well. Baptismal matters were more summarily dealt with in the *Constitution* itself,[4] and some of the most important aspects of baptismal theory and practice indeed appear in other conciliar documents altogether—documents which reflect less the concerns of advocates of liturgical reform than those of theologians dealing with ecclesiology in the dogmatic *Constitution on the Church*, and of missionaries concerned with sacramental adaptation to the needs of Christian formation in nonwestern cultures in the *Decree on the Missionary Activity of the Church*.[5] In view of this, one may not be too far wrong in judging baptismal reform as the "sleeper" among the sacramental and liturgical issues addressed by the Council; that is, the one which would emerge as perhaps that of most fundamental importance for the renewal of the Church as it gradually modulated into a new key after the Council completed its work in 1965.

The sequence taken by liturgical reform after 1965 illustrates this judgment. First priority was given to executing the Council's directions concerning eucharistic reform because of the central place held by the Mass in Catholic piety, and because historical and theological literature among Catholics was more fully developed on this topic. Promulgation of the actual reforms was gradual and elaborately cautious, marked by committee compromises forced largely by papal interventions and demands voiced in the first synod of bishops. A certain hypersensitivity concerning the Mass was thus instrumental in producing a compromised eucharistic rite that is perhaps the most uneven in both structure and general quality of the reformed rites that went into effect over the next decade. Other reformed rites attracted less attention, and being issued in a less compromised form are generally of better quality than that of the eucharist. The reform of the lectionary and of the liturgy of the hours has much to do with restoring a real piety of the Word in Catholic liturgical life, something no strategic renewal in the Church of the Word Incarnate can be without.

Yet the most mature of these reforms (partly because they were almost the last), and surely the most far-reaching in the renewal of Catholic life, has resulted not merely in the reform of baptism but in the complete overhaul of Catholic initiatory practice. This is contained in the rites for the baptism of children (1969), for confirmation (1971), and especially for the initiation of adults (1972).[6] Less compromised by hierarchical interventions during the process of their elaboration in the postconciliar committees (due partly to less sensitivity regarding baptism than the eucharist), these documents together represent significant shifts in Catholic initiation polity. As we have seen, many of these shifts stemmed from theoretical and practical research into baptism in its fullness that was in motion in European churches during the decade or so prior to 1959. The shifts were away from an initiatory polity dating from the sixteenth century and contained in the *Roman Ritual*. This book, first issued in 1614 and reflecting late medieval practice hardened by polemic with the Protestant Reformers, in fact if not in law made the normal rite of baptism that for the baptism of infants—a rite which amounted to a compression and truncation of the ancient Roman baptismal liturgy originally developed with adults in mind. Thus the rite which had once been the full liturgical context within which the texts for infant baptism could be accurately perceived had for all practical purposes vanished from use. Now even adult converts were regularly being initiated according to the abbreviated rite for infants. Although the full rite of adult baptism in a late medieval form remained in the *Roman Pontifical* after 1595, its great length and its being entirely in Latin assured that it would be used only in the rarest of cases.[7] Doubtless many parish clergy were hardly aware of its existence.

Given this state of affairs, the postconciliar subcommission charged with reforming the rites of Christian initiation, headed by Balthasar Fischer of Trier, proceeded with a series of wide consultations involving theologians, liturgical scholars, catechists, missionaries, and pastors from 1967 through 1970. The distillation of their findings is to be seen in the introductions to the three initiatory documents mentioned above, the last of which was to be that of the *Rite of Christian Initiation of Adults* in 1972.[8] This rite, emerging at the end of a long process of research, consultation, and collating reactions to the previously issued rites of baptism for children and confirmation by bishops, was thus the last and most mature outcome of the postconciliar subcommission's work. Its intent was to be a preparation not merely for the final sacramental *rites* of initiation (baptism-confirmation-eucharist), but for a *life of faith* in which asceticism, good works, and sacramental engagement could blend in a robust whole rather than languish as mere options, supine before the idiosyncracies of personal taste and piety.

The liturgical reforms contained in the *Rite of Christian Initiation of Adults* thus quite transcend the tactical alterations in rubrics many people came to expect of postconciliar efforts toward modernizing Catholic worship. Wisely noting that when one attempts to give ritual structure to so complex a process as conversion and coming to faith nothing can be determined *a priori*,[9] the document's purpose is less to give liturgical recipes than to shift the Church's initiatory polity from one conventional norm centering on infant baptism to the more traditional norm centering on adults. Nowhere does the document say this in so many words. If this is not the case, however, then the document not only makes no sense but is vain and fatuous. Its extensive and sensitive dispositions for gradually incorporating adult converts into communities of faith nowhere suggest that this process should be regarded as the rare exception. On the contrary, from deep within the Roman tradition it speaks of the process presumptively as normative.

THE NORM OF EUCHARIST

An analogy may help in grasping this fundamental principle, which the document assumes without giving reasons or arguments. The Second Vatican Council, in law being considered ecumenical and thus functioning with supreme power in the Church,[10] was concerned with reasserting strategic polities—not with pleading causes or descending into the intricacies of tactical reforms by which its reasserted polities might be given practical life. The latter task was left to the enabling work of postconciliar commissions such as that on the liturgy, whose mandate was to implement the orientations on worship contained in the *Constitution on the Sacred Liturgy* and other conciliar documents. The former task, that of pleading and explaining causes, was left to apologetes, scholars, and pastors. The method of conciliar reform through legislation begins therefore with assertions of the tradition and is expected to filter down through commissions enjoined to render traditional theory practical on the local level. The hope is that the reforms so achieved might catalyze day-to-day Christian living in such a way that a qualitative renewal of that life will occur.

Two of the fundamental norms asserted by the Council in its *Constitution on the Sacred Liturgy* had to do with baptism and eucharist, the two premier New Testament sacraments, the hinges upon which the whole sacramental order of Catholic tradition swings. Concerning the eucharist, the Council reasserted that its normal performance is to be seen in that of the bishop presiding within an event that concretely expresses the full involvement of the whole local church—people, presbyters, deacons and other assistants.[11] The norm requires that the Church be palpably manifested in all its splendid variety and ministerial diversity in all its sacramental deeds—but especially in eucharistic celebrations, which are the mode in which the Church itself most regularly assembles. The norm means not that the bishop must preside at every Mass, even if this were possible. It does mean, however, that in both theory and practice the eucharist is never to be regarded as anything less than an act of the whole Church, head and members, and that this *norm* must to some extent always be achieved, even when the chief pastor of the local church does not himself preside. The eucharist is never a matter of a bishop's or presbyter's own feelings or piety alone: it is never "his Mass." Nor is the sacrifice of the New Covenant ever merely a matter of contractual obligation between private parties in the Church. Rather, it is always the Church being most itself in public, obedient to the Lord's command to "do this for my remembrance," in a manner worthy of his Body at once ecclesial and sacramental.

Underlying this eucharistic norm is a wholly crucial theology of faith that is actualized constantly in communal events both sacramental in nature and ecclesial in scope. No event that may occur apart from this norm, no matter how usual or frequent, can be anything but abnormal to some degree. No event that occurs in opposition to it can be anything less than materially schismatic, no matter how pious the motive or good the intention, because it ruptures that corporate communion in faith of which the eucharist is simultaneously the ultimate sacramental sign and cause.

A *norm* in this sense has nothing to do with the number of times a thing is done, but it has everything to do with the standard according to which a thing is done. So long as the norm is in place both in practice and in the awareness of those who are engaged in it, the situation is capable of being judged "normal" even though the norm must be departed from to some extent, even frequently, due to exigencies of time, place, pastoral considerations, physical inabilities, or whatever. Yet to the extent possible, the norm must always be achieved to some extent lest it slip imperceptibly into the status of a mere "ideal" all wish for but are under no obligation to realize. Similar to a constitutional principle in law, such as the right to trial by a jury of one's peers (a principle which may be departed from in specific instances without nullifying the principle), a conciliar norm is not a restriction of freedom but an assertion of the specific breadth a freedom has to be robustly exercised within a given society. Societies being neither general nor abstract, their norms exist to secure a condition of stability congruent with the nature and ends of the societies themselves. Norms focus freedom in society for the common good as defined by social contract. They also enable the society to reach a degree of common consensus not only on the difference between what is normal and abnormal in its life, but also on the degrees of abnormality it can sustain as benign or must avoid as pathological to its own survival as a group. Norms are where style is born, and style is the way one society can be distinguished from another in its day-to-day existence.

THE NORM OF BAPTISM

The norm of baptism was stated by the Council in a more diffused form than that of the eucharist, but no less definitely, to be solemn sacramental initiation done especially at the paschal vigil and preceded by a catechumenate of serious content and considerable duration. This implies strongly, even if it does not require, that the initiate be an adult or at least a child well advanced in years.[12] The conciliar emphasis is clearly on the adult nature of the norm of Christian initiation, deriving as it does from the New Testament doctrine of conversion.[13] Although there is nowhere in the acts of the Council the slightest denigration of infant baptism, there is also no suggestion that the baptism of infants represents the norm of Catholic tradition. Equally, the Council nowhere suggests that the initiation of adults should be regarded either as exceptional or abnormal.

In this, the normal as defined by tradition is differentiated from the usual as defined by convention. The notion that infant baptism must be regarded as something less than normal cannot set easily with many Catholics, lay as well as clerical, who have never known anything else. But its abnormality does not require one to conclude that it is illegitimate: tradition clearly seems to know the baptism of infants from the beginning. But tradition with equal clarity does *not* know one thing often implied by the conventional frequency of infant baptism, namely, that baptism in infancy is the normal manner in which one becomes a Catholic Christian. Tradition's witness to the baptism of adults as the norm throws infant baptism into perspective as a benign abnormality so long as it is practiced with prudence as an unavoidable pastoral necessity—in situations such as the frail health of the infant, or in response to the earnest desire of Christian parents whose faith is vigorous and whose way of life gives clear promise that their child will develop in the faith of the Church. But at the same time, tradition's witness to adult baptism as the norm provides a solid counterbalance against infant baptism's becoming a malign abnormality due to pastoral malfeasance, theological obsession, or the decline of faith among Christian parents into some degree of merely social conformity. The data of neither scripture nor tradition can be made to support infant baptism as the pastoral norm. But those same data clearly support the practice as a benign abnormality in the life of a community whose ministry regularly focuses upon the evangelization, catechesis, and initiation of adults of faith into its midst. Initiatory normality in this sense provides the richest pastoral and theological milieu within which infant baptism can be ascertained for what it really ought to be in the life of the Church—not an unremembered substitute for conversion in faith, but a modest manifestation of God's love for all ages and of the stunning liberality of his grace, especially in difficult circumstances.

The Council's concern was to reiterate that the Church continually comes into existence in and through the full rhythm of Christian initiation, the normal scope of which is to be seen in the *Rite of Christian Initiation of Adults*. So radical is baptism that it is not merely something the Church may do in its spare time. In one sense the Church does not precede baptism; baptism precedes the Church. "In explicit terms, [Christ] himself affirmed the necessity of faith and baptism (Mk. 16:16, Jn. 3:5) and thereby affirmed also the necessity of the Church, for through baptism as through a door men enter the Church."[14] This entry does not begin in the waters of the font but with entry into the catechumenate: "Catechumens who, moved by the Holy Spirit, seek with explicit intention to be incorporated into the Church are by that very intention joined to her. With love and solicitude Mother Church already embraces them as her own."[15] From the first moment of the converting, one's emergent faith being discerned as requiring corporate participation, the individual is to be regarded as joined to the Church, as already having begun to be a Christian, if not yet one of the baptized *fideles*.

This concept, which is a salient part of the Council's norm of baptism, is perhaps even more unfamiliar to most Catholics than the notion of infant baptism's being an abnormality. Yet it is anything but novel. It represents sustained patristic teaching exemplified as early as Hippolytus: "If anyone being a catechumen should be apprehended for the Name, let him not be anxious about undergoing martyrdom. For if he suffer violence and be put to death before baptism, he shall be justified having been baptized in his own blood."[16] The convert's intent to be joined to the Church in baptism has already begun to take ecclesial form in his or her very engagement in the catechumenate. The catechumen has assumed a definite role in the Church as witness to conversion in Jesus Christ. The scope of this role is as real as it is extensive, as the *Decree on the Missionary Activity of the Church* makes clear: ". . . Christian initiation through the catechumenate should be taken care of not only by catechists or priests, but by the entire community of the faithful, especially by the sponsors. Thus, right from the outset the catechumens will feel that they belong to the People of God. . . . For since they are joined to the Church, they are already of the household of Christ."[17]

This requires modification of the assumption which has accompanied the conventional spread of *quamprimum* infant baptism that not to be baptized means that one is a non-Christian at best or a pagan at worst. It means that a catechumen is a Christian and a member of the ecclesial community both local and universal. As a group catechumens occupy a place intrinsic to Church life not only because they are recipients of the faith in a passive way through the teaching they are given. They also possess definite if limited rights—to the liturgy of the Word, to Christian burial, and they may even contract sacramental marriage prior to their actual baptism.[18] Of even more importance, however, catechumens together form a corporate presence that discharges a true ministry in the Church by witnessing constantly to the Church her need for continuing conversion in Christ. In this catechumens share in the building up of the Church along with other corporate groups or *orders* in the Church such as the order of the Faithful and the orders of ordained ministries (deacons, presbyters, and bishops).

The Council's reassertion of the norm of baptism as embracing the order of catechumens restores to the Church a structure of vital importance by which the orders just mentioned may discover themselves afresh. In addition, the presence of catechumens in a local church must inevitably evoke a clearer awareness of the important gifts and services to the Church on the part of evangelists and catechists, and an awareness that the cultivation of their gifts is best done not in isolation but in corporate groups where insights and techniques can be shared, policies formulated, and problems dealt with. The catechumenate may thus spur diversification of formal nonclerical ministries in the Church quite beyond what the less "ordered," more informal, and largely honorific function of special ministers of communion can be expected to accomplish. Without a catechumenate it is difficult to foresee what factors could call into existence a ministerial order of catechists that would deal with conversion instead of religious education in school classrooms, or a ministerial order of evangelists that would take the proclamation of the gospel into places where ordained clergy cannot easily go. Moreover, the Church needs the corporate witness of such orders *as groups* within the ecclesial body politic at least as much as it needs their day-to-day services—services that may have been in fact performed by many in the Church through recent centuries but without recognition, continuity, status, or the *esprit de corps* required.[19]

Restoration of the order of catechumens may also throw new light on the place of penance in the Church's life. The ancient order of penitents developed out of and in close analogy to the *prima paenitentia* of catechumenal preparation for baptism. Catechumens were elected for Easter baptism at the beginning of Lent; so too, penitents were designated for sacramental reconciliation in the Church on Holy Thursday just before Lent began by an imposition of ashes and sackcloth—a practice that has become Ash Wednesday. Thus both catechumens and penitents doing *secunda paenitentia* moved through Lent in corporate tandem as orders of persons who visibly witnessed to the ascetical demands of faith in local churches at each liturgical assembly in the midst of the Faithful. The entire local church thus had immediate access to practical manifestations of the costs of faith each year as it prepared for the premier celebration of its own faith in the events of Christ's passion, death, and resurrection during the *pascha*. All that had happened long ago became actual not just in the local church's memory but in the souls and bodies of those for whom the church expended such love, care, and prayer during the whole of Lent—its catechumens and penitents.

The very spirit of this discipline perhaps makes uneasy those today who have become accustomed to religion as a private affair. Sequestering catechumens into private inquiry classes renders them anonymous to the Church, rather as sequestering penitents into private confession and penance both subjectivizes the notion of sin and disperses a sense of community reponsibility for it. Each development results equally in privatizing the sacraments of baptism and reconciliation, thus removing from church structure and awareness two of the most effective corporate witnesses to repentance and conversion. Such lack of public witness does not deny the effects of baptism and penance upon the individuals who "receive" them, but it warps reflection on the effects baptism and penance have *upon the Church which baptizes and reconciles*. In removing the corporate witness of catechumens and penitents from the Church's day-to-day consciousness, the same polity impedes the Church's regular access to God's Word as the sole dependable criterion for Christian life and behavior. For that Word can be heard for what it is only in conversion and repentance, as both scripture and tradition insist. Failing this, the Church too easily slips into using precedents and criteria for ordering its life that have either little to do with the gospel or fall beneath its judgment. The whole tenor of the Council's many documents bears witness to its opinion that renewal does not lie in this direction.

THE PASTORAL ROOTS OF THE NORM OF BAPTISM

From all this at least two things are clear. The first is that, again, the Council's norm of baptism embraces more than just the sacramental water bath alone. It extends back into the whole process by which faith is conceived in an individual through evangelization, nurtured by catechesis to a point of maturity that can bear public sharing, sealed by the tripartite sacramental event of baptism-confirmation-eucharist, and (as we shall see) brought to a certain cognitive and emotional term in postbaptismal catechesis or mystagogy. The whole sequence is Church-wide not merely in theory but in practice. Furthermore, its ramifications are so multivalent as to suggest that the sequence, sustained throughout the year and reaching its peak in the annual rhythms of Lent and the celebration of Easter, constitutes the Church's radical business for the good of the world itself. The whole process is a closely articulated whole, each part of which relates to all the others, and no one of which can afford to float free either in theory or practice. The whole is baptism in its fullness, the making of a Christian, the ongoing birth of the Church of Jesus Christ in his life-giving Spirit.[20]

The second thing is that this norm of baptism has its origins not in the theories of pedants dreaming in academe but is rooted in the pastoral memory and awareness of the Roman Church. It grew out of the pastoral circumstances of that gathering of movements which was primitive Christianity as it faced appalling challenges. The diversity of initiatory practices in the various churches remained the rule for centuries, as we have seen, and has never been eliminated to this day.[21] One reason for this is that there never was a single unanimous account of the

Lord's baptizing in the New Testament as there was for the eucharist—a rite which, for all its apparent diversity in development, remains consistently more firm and discernible in structure across time and from church to church than does baptism. There was a Last Supper, but no Last Baptism that has been recorded. Furthermore, while the plurality of baptismal norms among the several most ancient churches may well be apostolic in itself, there is no apostolic authority for baptism's being accomplished in nothing but the water event without accompanying rites, nor is it probable that such a thing ever existed.[22]

Another reason for the tenacity of baptismal particularity in historic churches such as the Roman must be that the working out of a church's norm of baptism was done under enormous, and thus memorable, pastoral stress. This would have been especially so during the first three centuries, when hostility to Christianity from many quarters was common. But even from the fourth to the sixth century, particularly from 330 to 460, though the empire was rapidly becoming Christian, pastoral stresses intensified as they changed in kind. Theological reflection was beginning to reach its first synthesis; pastoral activity was rapidly reaching a series of accommodations with a more benign milieu; the Christian vision was pumping new life into old things and creating new things throughout the known world.[23] In particular during those 130 years—a space of some four generations from the death of Eusebius to the death of Leo the Great—almost every major church father with the exception of Origen was alive and at work. Indeed, during Augustine's own lifetime from 354 to 430 no less than Ambrose, Jerome, Basil, Gregory of Nyssa, Gregory of Nazianzus, John Chrysostom, Cyril of Jerusalem, Theodore of Mopsuestia, and Cyril and

Athanasius of Alexandria were all active, and all but Jerome were bishops of local churches.

Faced as they were in their local churches with absorbing increasingly large numbers of adult converts whose motives were often politics and fashion rather than faith, these pastors expanded and developed the sort of primitive catechesis that can still be read in the first six chapters of the *Didache* into a body of reflection on corporate faith through conversion and sacramental enactment that was meant to sustain Christian fidelity beneath such a flood. The sophistication of this catechetical development can be seen by comparing the *Didache* chapters with the catechetical homilies of Cyril of Jerusalem (c. 347), John Chrysostom (386–398), and with Augustine's *De Catechizandis Rudibus* (c. 405).[24] It amounts to a richly pastoral theology, worked out among one's colleagues in faith gathered for worship rather than out of books by teachers in seminaries and colleges. Based on God's Word proclaimed in sessions with adult catechumens and in eucharistic assemblies of the Faithful on Sunday mornings, its core is the pain-filled ambiguity of conversion in faith shared among people struggling to keep the gospel without succumbing to their own astounding evangelical success.

Yet one should not romanticize the era, despite the real accomplishments it witnessed. The civilized world was beginning, implacably, to break down. Chrysostom was to die in exile from his see, his cathedral church ruined by arson. The fathers' congregations were likely no more sensitive or well-educated than now, nor were there fewer whose attitude toward the faith might be described as one of "respectful undisbelief" than in our own day.[25] Augustine complained that they chatted all during his sermons, and that they stank so badly in the August heat of North Africa that he sometimes had to leave the building.

What emerged nonetheless from this engagement by bishops in the catechumenal process and carried over inevitably into the life of their churches on all levels was a vision of the Church, a pastoral ecclesiology, unsurpassed in its concrete sacramental realism. The sacraments were seen as a totality coextensive with the Church's life itself, a life carried on in a series of events which arose out of and in turn shaped all the members of the local church—catechumens, penitents, inquirers, clergy, and Faithful. The liturgy was seen not as a matter of exquisite ecclesiastical ceremonial to occupy clergy and religious but as the way a Christian people live in common. Whatever such a people did *as* a people was liturgical, an act of corporate worship of God. What this act meant was sacramental—understood as any thing or act that relates one to God.[26] And the whole consummated the Church's mission, a mission perceived above all else as to be the corporate living presence of God's tough but graceful pleasure in Jesus Christ for the world.

To enter such a corporate body, the fathers thought, required the most careful discernment of intentions in the convert and a briskly aggressive initiatory polity on the churches' part. Without these it would be questionable whether such a people's mutual union could rise even to a minimal level of sacramental expression. In such a case one would be dealing with an insuperable pastoral anomaly: eucharistized catechumens at best or baptized pagans at worst. Nothing could rise on such a foundation. Baptism would not be the first major ecclesial outcome of conversion in faith; the eucharist would have no communion in faith to celebrate; the gospel would be reduced to a mere catalogue of gnostic secrets or a clot of problems for scholars to dispute; the sacraments would have no faith-content to relate; the liturgy would be a mere pomp even less benign than the pagans' "gestures charged with soul," leaving the individual culturally deracinated and isolated amid the searing truths of a vertiginous monotheism. The Church itself would have little reason to exist, much less a mission in the world to accomplish.

Tertullian had already observed that Christians are not born but made. Augustine and his colleagues over a century later would have agreed, perhaps extending the epigram to say that they do not just wander in off the streets either. They are honed down by the teaching and discipline of the catechumenate until their metal is tough, resilient, sharp, and glowing. The "enlightenment" of baptism was not a flickering flame but a burst of God's glory in those whose capacities to receive it had been expanded to their utmost.[27] And although things were different since the pagan Celsus had written archly in 168 that "If all men wanted to be Christian, the Christians would no longer want them,"[28] being prepared in the fifth century to absorb a whole society did not mean that the churches would do so indiscriminately. The fathers' catechetical homilies suggest that they still needed more Christians less than they needed better ones, even as they wished and worked for the conversion of all. The memory of the martyrs, for example, was still so strong that their popular cult threatened to quite disrupt the good order of Augustine's church, and whole provinces in the west remained strongly pagan. Yet he and his colleagues were not prepared to allow their evangelical desires to degenerate into vague benevolence or slack initiatory practice. Even less was their desire for better Christians allowed to become an arrogant elitism of the saved. This was precisely what they criticized gnostics and sectarians for, and it was the genesis of their coming to call the Church "catholic"—total, whole, and meant for all.

The Church in all it is and does was perceived to be splendidly varied yet one. There was no thought that it came into existence only at the Sunday eucharist or only in charitable work among the poor. Rather, these events were the inevitable and interlocking results of living in a communion of faith shared beneath the judgment of God's Word and in the Lord's Spirit. Shaping people to live this way and supporting them in their doing so was the Christian community's most pressing business. It began in the catechumenate, a structure in which one's conversion could be brought to a point strong enough to endure the sharing of one's faith in common. The way this took place was through the conversion therapy of catechesis and through sacramental initiation. *Catechesis* was understood to be not about education but about conversion. *Conversion* was perceived to be not about doctrinal formulations so much as about coming to faith as a way of living together in Jesus Christ become a Spirit-laden people. *Sacramental initiation* was known to be a whole sequence that began in water and oil and was consummated in one's first eucharistic communion, a sequence that was about membership—the full, active, and conscious participation in such a people and all its deeds.[29] Put briefly, catechesis was not thought to be merely instructional; it was conversion therapy for corporate membership through sacramental illumination.[30] By the same token, the sacraments of initiation were not thought to be merely a set of three separate religious rites designed to mark the individual's natural stages of psychological growth. Rather, they were a unified sacramental discipline through which both convert *and* community moved in the Spirit from what each had been toward what each was capable of becoming under grace in that same Spirit—a movement shot through with both pain and glory, with affirmation and renunciation, exorcism and celebration toward a new degree of communion in faith that would leave both convert *and* community irrevocably changed. And all this constituted the heartbeat of that new creation which the fathers perceived the Church to be.

The *Rite of Christian Initiation of Adults* thus presents a most traditional norm of baptismal polity in the Roman Catholic Church for today. Its concern has less to do with answers to specific problems than with a coherent vision of how communion in faith might more adequately be lived in a pastoral context that in many ways bears a close similarity to that which gave rise to the traditional norm in the first place. Its desire, moreover, is not to provide liturgical recipes but to deal with the perennial *Lebensprobleme* that lie at the root of Christian communality in all its aspects—liturgical, ethical, doctrinal, ministerial, and ecclesial. Its purpose is to reenforce where possible and recreate where needed the insights and structures that are capable of integrating facets of ecclesial life which strayed apart from each other in the past for a variety of reasons.

Some, even many, of the *Rite's* ceremonial details may with use be found to be expendable. But its perceptive vision of the radical unity of the faith lived in communion with God among all his holy ones and by all his holy things constitutes an irreducible norm that wells up out of the deepest springs of the Roman Church's own apostolic tradition. Far more than mere uniformity, this unity is *economia*—an elemental theological phenomenon that involves the theandric richness of compenetrating relationships sustained by divine initiative and faithful human response.

Rather as the Father is known in the Son, and as the Church is known only in its being the palpable locale of the Spirit to whom the mutual love of Son and Father gives rise; so too the distinct but inseparable elements in ecclesial life together are known only in the illumination one element throws upon the other, discovering there the meaning of itself.

The *Rite's* norm of baptism thus rests on the economic principle that baptism is inadequately perceptible apart from the eucharist; that the eucharist is not wholly knowable without reference to conversion in faith; that conversion is abortive if it does not issue in sacramental illumination by incorporation into the Church; that the Church is only an inept corporation without steady access to Sunday, Lent, and the Easter Vigil; that evangelization is mere noise and catechesis only a syllabus apart from conversion and initiation into a robust ecclesial environment of faith shared. In baptism the eucharist begins, and in the eucharist baptism is sustained. From this premier sacramental union flows all the Church's life.

NOTES

1. Some major work was published or in preparation in Germany during this same time, e.g., Alois Stenzel, *Die Taufe: eine genetische Erklärung der Taufliturgie* (Verlag Felizian Rauch, Innsbruck 1958); Burkhard Neunheuser, *Baptism and Confirmation*, trans. J. J. Hughes (Herder and Herder, New York 1964).

2. See, for example, his *The American Parish and the Roman Liturgy* (Macmillan, New York 1958) and *H.A.R.: The Autobiography of Father Reinhold*, with foreword by W. H. Auden (Herder and Herder, New York 1968).

3. Para. 47-58 (Abbott 154-157).

4. Para. 64-68 (Abbott 159-160).

5. See the *Constitution on the Church* 14 (Abbott 32-33) and the *Decree on the Missionary Activity of the Church* 13-14 (Abbott 599-601), concerning catechumens and the catechumenate. Also the *Decree on the Pastoral Office of Bishops (Christus Dominus)* 14 (Abbott 406) and the *Decree on the Ministry and Life of Priests (Presbyterorum Ordinis)* 6 (Abbott 543-546).

6. *Rite of Baptism for Children* (United States Catholic Conference, Washington, D.C. 1969); *Rite of Confirmation* (National Conference of Catholic Bishops: Bishops' Committee on the Liturgy, Washington, D.C. 1972); *Rite of Christian Initiation of Adults* (United States Catholic Conference, Washington, D.C. 1974).

7. In 1866 even the stages of the catechumenate reflected in the adult rite, and their attempted adaptation to cultural patterns by missionaries in China, were condemned and suppressed as an "abuse" by a curial document. See J. Christiaens, "L'organisation d'un catéchuménat au XVIe siècle," *La Maison-Dieu* 58 (1959) 71-82, especially 81.

8. The subcommission responsible for the *Rite* was headed by Jacques Cellier of Paris. See André Aubry, "Le projet pastoral du rituel de l'initiation des adultes," *Ephemerides Liturgicae* 88 (1974) 174-191.

9. Para. 20.

10. Canon 228, para. 1: *Concilium Oecumenicum suprema pollet in universam Ecclesiam potestate.*

11. *Constitution on the Sacred Liturgy* 41-42 (Abbott 152-153).

12. See notes 4 and 5, above.

13. For example, see the *Decree on the Missionary Activity of the Church* 13 (Abbott 599-600).

14. The dogmatic *Constitution on the Church* 14 (Abbott 32).

15. Ibid. (Abbott 33).

16. *Apostolic Tradition* 19 (Whitaker 3-4).

17. Para. 14 (Abbott 601). So too Augustine, *In Joannis Evangelium Tractatus* 11:4 (Migne, *P.L.* 35:1476).

18. *Rite of Christian Initiation of Adults* 24. See too canons 1149, 1152, and 1234 para. 2.

19. See Aidan Kavanagh, "Ministries in the Community and the Liturgy," *Liturgy: Self-Expression of the Church*, Concilium Series 72 (Herder and Herder, New York 1972) 55-67.

20. See the *Decree on the Ministry and Life of Priests* 2 and 5 (Abbott 533-536, 541-543); *Decree on the Church's Missionary Activity* 14 (Abbott 600-601); *Constitution on the Liturgy* 71 (Abbott 169). The apostolic constitution of Paul VI on confirmation, *Divinae consortium naturae*, published 15 August 1971, stresses the unity of Christian initiation. See also P.-M. Gy, "The Idea of 'Christian Initiation,'" *Studia Liturgica* 12:2/3 (1977) 172-175.

21. See the essay by G. Kretschmar, "Recent Research on Christian Initiation," *Studia Liturgica* 12:2/3 (1977) 87-106.

22. Thus Kretschmar 103.

23. See Peter Brown, *The World of Late Antiquity* (Thames and Hudson, London 1971) 82-94, 115-125.

24. *St. Cyril of Jerusalem's Lectures on the Christian Sacraments*, ed. F. L. Cross (SPCK, London 1966); *St. John Chrysostom: Baptismal Instructions*, ed. P. W. Harkins, Ancient Christian Writers Series 31 (Westminster Publishing Company, Westminster, Maryland 1963); *St. Augustine: The First Catechetical Instruction*, ed. J. P. Christopher (Regnery Logos Books, Chicago 1966). See also *The Awe-Inspiring Rites of Initiation: Baptismal Homilies of the Fourth Century*, ed. Edward Yarnold (St. Paul Publications, Slough, England 1971); F. van der Meer, *Augustine the Bishop*, trans. B. Battershaw and G. R. Lamb (Sheed and Ward, New York 1961) especially 453-467. For the most thorough study in English, see Hugh Riley, *Christian Initiation: A Comparative Study of the Interpretation of the Baptismal Liturgy in the Mystagogical Writings of Cyril of Jerusalem, John Chrysostom, Theodore of Mopsuestia, and Ambrose of Milan* (Catholic University of America Press, Washington, D.C. 1974).

25. The phrase is John Meagher's in *The Gathering of the Ungifted* (Herder-Seabury, New York 1973).

26. See F. van der Meer 279-285.

27. The statement of P.-M. Gy, in "The Idea of 'Christian Initiation,'" *Studia Liturgica* 12:2/3 (1977), 175, that in antiquity "It is baptism itself which illuminates and initiates, much more than catechesis," is true. But it should not be read as a denigration of catechesis: the quantity and caliber of the fathers' catechetical works belie this. Rather, baptism so subordinated catechesis that the latter became part of the very process of baptismal illumination and initiation. Baptism was anything but an act wholly separate from catechesis and in opposition to it.

28. Quoted in Brown 82.

29. See Aidan Kavanagh, "What is Participation?" *Doctrine and Life* 23 (1973) 343-353.

30. See Aidan Kavanagh, "Teaching Through the Liturgy," *Notre Dame Journal of Education* 5:1 (1974) 35-47.

Chapter Five

The Reforms of the Second Vatican Council: The Rites of Adult Initiation

The *Rite of Christian Initiation of Adults* was first published as *Ordo Initiationis Christianae Adultorum* by the Sacred Congregation for Divine Worship in January of 1972.[1] The Latin typicum is a document of 185 pages that contains the full rites of adult initiation,[2] a simpler form of the same rites for use in exceptional circumstances such as illness,[3] and an abbreviated form for use in danger of death.[4] Three other matters are also included: 1) directions for confirmation and first communion for adults who were validly baptized as infants or young children, but who never received adequate catechesis later;[5] 2) rites of initiation for children of older age who were never baptized as infants;[6] and 3) rites for the admission into full communion with the Roman Catholic Church of those who have already been validly baptized in another communion.[7] In addition, a repertoire of various optional texts and readings for use in the celebration of adult initiation is provided.[8]

The General Introduction to all the reformed initiatory rites, including the Baptism of Children and Confirmation by Bishops, makes it clear that the premier rite is that of full initiation of adults. All the other initiatory rites fall into their proper place under its aegis, and their various details often refer back to the full rite of adult initiation as the governing norm of them all. Because of this, the spirit and principles contained in the full rites of adult initiation are operative throughout the other initiatory rites: the former subordinate the latter as soul subordinates body, as function subordinates form. In the most practical way, therefore, the full rites of adult initiation give shape, articulation, and fundamental continuity of meaning to all the other rites which constitute the Roman initiatory economy.

This represents the most crucial restoration contained in the document—a restoration in the way Roman Catholicism thinks about the whole of sacramental reality. Rather than regarding the sacraments as separate entities, each containing a meaning exclusive to itself and apart from all others, the full rites of adult initiation presume that all the initiatory rites form one closely articulated whole which relates intimately with all the other noninitiatory sacraments and rites. The entire sacramental economy is thus viewed not as something divorced from and peripheral to Church life, but as the very way in which that life is lived in common and on the most crucial level. The vision is one in which a sacramental theology and an ecclesiology mate to become functions of one another, producing in the concrete a church order of a particular (in this case Roman) kind. Sacraments are a realized ecclesiology in time and place, according to definite cultural rhythms and specific theological accents. The Church may be universal, but it is neither abstract nor always univocal in expression.

The importance of the restored rites of adult initiation lies therefore less in its ceremonial details than in its strategic vision of the Church local and universal. It is a practicable vision of what the Church is and can become through the continuing renewal process of evangelization, conversion, catechesis, and the paschal sacraments of Christian initiation.

THE STRUCTURE OF THE RITES OF ADULT INITIATION

The full rites for the initiation of adults include not only the closely articulated sacraments of baptism, confirmation, and eucharist [208-234], but also the rites of the catechumenate. Preceding these are ample explanations of the catechumenal phases of the initiation process [4-67]. These preparatory explanations are not only welcome but also necessary, since by far the largest part of the initiatory sequence centers on the catechumenate [68-207]. The catechumenate is here regarded as an ecclesial and liturgical structure within which conversion therapy is carried on. Catechesis is understood to be concerned with conversion in Christ and with how to live continuously in such a manner not only prior to but after initiation as well. As such, "The initiation of catechumens takes place step by step in the midst of the community of the faithful. Together with the catechumens the faithful reflect upon the value of the paschal mystery, renew their own conversion, and by their example lead the catechumens to obey the Holy Spirit more generously"[4].

That the formation of catechumens takes place sequentially "in the midst of the community of the faithful" accounts for the several stages or steps being given a liturgical form and style. In this way catechesis is thrown open to the whole local church as a cycle of worship events that focuses upon the critical issues of conversion in faith and renewal of life not only for individuals but for the entire ecclesial community as well. Catechumens are viewed not as anonymous attendants at private educational inquiry classes, but as public persons in the local church. Their faith, progress, and prognosis in communal faith-living are the concerns of the entire local church met for solemn public worship. Catechesis and all it touches are less the preserve of religious educators than they are the right and property of the Church of God.

EVANGELIZATION AND PRECATECHUMENATE [9-13]

While the rite of initiation properly so-called begins formally with admission to the catechumenate, stages preliminary to this are regarded as critically important for what is to follow. These preliminary stages are referred to variously as a time for "making inquiry" and for investigation and maturation of purpose on the part of the seeker. On the part of the local church this is a time of establishing trust and communication with the inquirer, of evangelizing the seeker by proclaiming "the living God . . . [and] Jesus Christ, whom he sent for the salvation of all." [9]. By living well its own life of faith, the local church has not only attracted those of open hearts to itself: it has also taken on obligations to such persons as well. In this initial and preformal dialectic between inquirer and local church a certain incipient but real communion with God and Christ in the Spirit has already been born. The solid theological reality of this communion, however potential and incipient it may yet be, stamps what follows with the mark of necessity rather than of vaguely recommended convenience. For faith as seen in the document is not merely a benevolent disposition nor a sincere anguish over the state of the world and the elusiveness of truth. Faith is seen as a concrete commitment of one's soul and body to the society of those who know Jesus Christ and him alone to be "the way, the truth and the life."

THE CATECHUMENATE [14-20]

Only the foregoing gives grounds for the document to say that "The rite of becoming a catechumen is of very great importance" [14]. It presupposes that the candidates for membership in the catechumenate are already grounded in the basics of "initial spiritual life and Christian teaching" a solid desire for ecclesial faith, and repentance together with a will to change one's life on entering into prayerful relationship with God in Christ among believing people [15]. Assembling publicly before the local church for the first time, "the candidates make their intention known to the Church; the Church, *carrying out its apostolic mission*, admits those who intend to become members" [14].[9] The point is of theological moment since admission to the catechumenate is characterized as an act of the Church's apostolic function. This means that admission to the catechumenate is not a preliminary formality of little or no ecclesiological or sacramental importance. The wording of [14] suggests the contrary, namely, that the *membership spoken of as being the result of this apostolic act on the Church's part is not the result of baptism but of being a catechumen*. Such membership is ecclesial because it aggregates one into a whole set of personal and structural relationships that are public and sacramental in nature; that is, the whole catechumenal structure that follows.

On admission their names are inscribed in the register of catechumens [17], and henceforth the catechumens are regarded as Christians. Although not yet members of the Faithful (this comes only with the sacramental sequence of baptism-confirmation-eucharist), catechumens occupy an overt place in Church structure and discharge a real ministry to the Church by witnessing in their own lives to the never-ending need of conversion in Christ that is requisite for the whole Church, universal as well as local. What the restatement of this traditional principle will do to the practice of infant baptism remains to be seen, but it is likely that the practice will not remain unaffected by it indefinitely.

The catechumenate is ordinarily to last "several years," and its content is described in [19] as consisting in pastoral formation accomplished through "suitable discipline." What is to be discerned in the catechumen during this period is not so much intellectual adequacy regarding concepts having to do with faith, but maturation in those dispositions toward the faith that were already manifest when the individual was admitted to the catechumenate. The maturation process is to be actively helped by the whole local church in four ways.

First, there is doctrinal formation by presbyters, deacons, catechists, and other professionally competent lay persons to enable the catechumens to attain a "suitable knowledge of dogmas and precepts" and an "intimate understanding of the mystery of salvation" [19: 1]. This formation is *to be accommodated to the liturgical year* and *enriched by seasonal celebrations of the Word*—which implies that what is envisaged is not merely a classroom effort in watered-down theology but a well rounded formation program that is suffused with a strong liturgical methodology. The document is clear on the purpose of catechesis: it is to make Christians who have something to repent of and celebrate, and who know how to do both in common.

Second, catechumens are to be formed by living closely with others who know well the cost and advantages of a Christian way of life. The exemplary role of sponsors, godparents, and the whole local community of faith is paramount in this mode of formation. One learns how to fast, pray, repent, celebrate, and serve the good of one's neighbor less by being lectured on these matters than by close association with people who do these things with regular ease and flair [19:2].

Third, and rather as specification of the second way, the catechumens' regular participation in public worship eases them gently and over a considerable period of time into a sacramental way of life. "Ordinarily, however, when they are present in the assembly of the faithful, they should be dismissed in a friendly manner before the eucharistic celebration begins . . . ; they must await their baptism, which will bring them into the priestly people and depute them to participate in the Christian worship of the new covenant" [19:3]. This means that while catechumens are regarded as Christians, their not yet being "of the faithful" should be manifested visibly in the worshiping assembly. The dismissal of catechumens before the prayer of the faithful and preparation of the gifts may in addition serve as an effective nonverbal catechesis for the Faithful themselves on the awesome dignity of their own baptism. To emphasize the real importance of this act it will be necessary to evolve once again in the Roman Rite some ritual form of dismissal, perhaps with community prayer for the catechumens.[10]

Fourth, and finally, "Since the Church's life is apostolic, catechumens should also learn how to work actively with others to spread the Gospel and build up the Church by the testimony of their lives and profession of their faith" [19:4]. From this it is again obvious that catechesis in the sense meant by the document goes quite beyond the classroom and its instructional techniques. What is envisaged here is not formal religious education: it is the practice of social action both in evangelization and in the corporal and spiritual acts of mercy. The effects of such a program may well be at least as telling on the local church as on the catechumens.

The section on the catechumenate concludes by noting that in something as long-term, complex, and demanding as this nothing can be determined *a priori* [20]. The adequacy of a catechumenate as regards both the catechumens and the local church to which they belong depends not on static guidelines to policy but on the wisdom and integrity of those reponsible for setting the period of time and directing the discipline of the catechumenate. Those ultimately responsible in this case are said to be the bishop and, more generally, the episcopal conferences of the various nations.

PERIOD OF PURIFICATION
AND ENLIGHTENMENT [21-26]

When it appears to the satisfaction of all those immediately concerned (local clergy, catechists, sponsors and godparents) that a catechumen has attained by grace and effort a conversion of mind and life, a sufficient knowledge of Christian teaching, and a becoming sense of faith and charity, he or she may be elected by the local church to enter proximate preparation for the sacraments of initiation when next these are to be celebrated [22-24]. The period of preparation is called a time of purification and enlightenment [21]. It is described as a period of spiritual recollection more than catechesis and is intended to "purify minds and hearts by the examination of conscience and by repentance and also to enlighten by a deeper knowledge of Christ the Savior" [25]. This time coincides usually, if not always, with Lent—a season which in its ethos, liturgy, and choice of readings prepares for baptismal initiation on Holy Saturday and for reconciliation of penitents on Holy Thursday and Good Friday.

The liturgical structure given to the period of purification and enlightenment is very explicit in the document. The act of electing catechumens for sacramental initiation is said to belong to the whole local church, and it is to be done publicly after the homily at the main eucharistic celebration on the first Sunday in Lent [22, 139]. The elect are then publicly scrutinized on their intentions and exorcized[11] after the homily at the main eucharistic celebrations on the third, fourth, and fifth Sundays in Lent. They are also formally presented with the creed and the Lord's Prayer at public celebrations as convenient, being expected to "give each back" by publicly reciting them at a later service [25:1-2, 181-184].

On Holy Saturday the elect are instructed to rest from ordinary work if possible and to spend their time in prayer, recollection, and fasting. If there is a meeting of the elect that same day, some of the preparatory rites may be done—such as the profession of faith (the Nicene or Apostles' Creed), the *ephphetha* ceremony, the choosing of a Christian name if this is customary, and the anointing with the oil of catechumens.

THE SACRAMENTS OF INITIATION [27-36]

The sacraments of baptism, confirmation, and the eucharist together constitute "the final stage in which the elect come forward and, with their sins forgiven, are admitted into the people of God, receive the adoption of the sons of God and are led by the Holy Spirit into the promised fullness of time and, in the eucharistic sacrifice and meal, to the banquet of the Kingdom of God" [27]. While the document presupposes that all this will be done normally within the liturgy of the Easter Vigil [208], it notes that even when it takes place at some other time of the year "the celebration should be filled with the Easter spirit" [209].

The insistence on the Easter Vigil as the normal setting for Christian initiation is neither ecclesiastical nostalgia nor doctrinal wistfulness. There is simply no other time of the year, and certainly no other liturgical context, that serves as so rich a setting for sacramental initiation and its meaning. Not only are the initiates dying and rising in Christ as the Church commemorates his passage from death to life long ago. More importantly the initiates are entering into his corporate real presence which is the Church, where his passage from death and "this world" to life unbounded remains an ongoing reality that is the pivot on which the renewed cosmos turns. Only the Easter Vigil yields up an ecclesiology that is worthy of baptism. The constant separation of baptism from this paschal context heretofore has weakened the theology both of the Church and of Christian initiation—to the detriment of the Church's self-understanding, of the faithful Christian's sense of his or her individual identity, and of the whole Body's ministry in the world.

When the Easter Vigil "speaks" about initiation, it does so in terms that are a veritable evangelization of the cosmos. Fire, wind, wax, bees, light and darkness, water, oil, nakedness, bread, wine, aromas, tough and graceful words and gestures—all these stand as a context without which what happens to one entering corporate faith in Jesus Christ dead and rising is only partially perceptible. The being and acts of Christ himself can even become constricted without regular access to the full paschal sweep of God's purpose that was being revealed even before the incarnation occurred.[12] Because the discipline of Christian initiation is impoverished without regular access to this full sweep of God's intent and accomplishment in Jesus Christ, the Church becomes less than it is and may be—and so does the world, God's creature.

Some words are needed on the document's plan for the sacraments of initiation within the Easter Vigil.

After the homily the ministers, the elect, and their godparents go to the font or baptistry where an exhortation is given by the presiding minister and the litany of the saints is sung. Then the following order is observed:

1. Blessing of baptismal water [215-216];
2. Renunciation of evil [217] and
3. Anointing with the oil of catechumens, if these have not already been done [206-207 and 217-218];
4. Profession of faith [219];
5. Baptism by immersion or infusion [220-222];
6. Anointing with chrism *if* confirmation is deferred for some *special* reason [223-224];
7. Giving a white garment and candle [225-226];
8. Confirmation [227-231];
9. The paschal eucharist, beginning with the preparation of the gifts [232-234].

Several matters deserve comment. First, the placement of sacramental initiation after the homily and before the first eucharist of Easter day in reality makes all that precedes it an extensive pre-eucharistic liturgy of the Word that centers upon the candidates for baptism. The liturgy of the Word may thus tend to have more the character of a "theme mass" for the candidates, rather as funerals often seem to take on a thematic emphasis centering on the deceased's life. This is a mistake at least in emphasis. Neither the vigil nor a funeral (nor for that matter a wedding or an ordination) is a liturgy "for" someone. These are celebrations *of* the Church, *by* the Church, and *for* the Church under the criteria of the gospel. Keeping this in mind, and developing a sense of reticent reverence with regard to what must be said and what really should not be said, might give liturgical events more vitality and scope—thus allowing more of those present to participate better instead of feeling "shut out" from an event that has become too personally oriented and narrowed.

The placement of initiation after the homily may also force the liturgy of the Word to take on more the character of the candidates' final catechetical session than that of a true vigil of watch and prayer. Early historical evidence suggests that the vigil of Easter was precisely that—a *vigil* of watch and prayer in which readings were employed not to instruct the elect about baptism but to galvanize the Faithful in their intense wait for the Mother of Feasts to begin. The vigil may well have even been carried on by the *fideles* while the elect were being baptized in a place separate from the vigil assembly. Baptism *in camera* was then the rule due to the required nakedness of the candidates. This fact, as we have noted, would almost necessitate some kind of formal presentation of the newly baptized, now anointed and dressed, to the assembly of Faithful, who had been keeping vigil in the church while the baptisms were in progress. And it may be that the ritual demands of such a presentation of the neophytes to the Faithful were responded to by the senior baptizing minister (usually the bishop) with a solemn imposition of hands, public prayer, and a final anointing with aromatic chrism done amidst the Faithful and greeted by them with ovations. This may be the practical genesis of what would later be called confirmation. Hippolytus, the earliest witness to peculiarly Roman usage, as we have seen, suggests as much: "And so each one drying himself they shall now put on their clothes, and after this let them be together in the assembly." There follows a description of the bishop's laying hands on and anointing the neophytes, after which he exchanges with them the kiss of peace for the first time.[13] The point is not a major one, but it might be kept in mind lest confirmation continue to be regarded as more separate a sacrament, and of more or less moment, than it is.

A second matter is the reiterated recognition of baptism by immersion in the Roman Rite. "If baptism is by immersion of the whole body or of the head only, decency and decorum should prevail" [220].[14] The concern for decency and decorum would not be necessary unless the rubric envisions the possibility of total or partial immersion. Baptizing in this way would be a welcome development because it might help restore something of the crucial and extraordinary nature of baptism to the Church's consciousness, and some of that drastic robustness to baptismal symbolism which for too long has been enfeebled by symbolic minimalism, initiatory privacy, and the anonymity of the baptized.

A third and most important matter is what is done with confirmation. The document is clear on the point that confirmation should normally happen *immediately* after baptism and *within* the same liturgical event.

"According to the ancient practice maintained in the Roman liturgy, an adult is not to be baptized unless he receives confirmation immediately afterward, provided no serious obstacles exist. *This connection signifies the unity of the paschal mystery, the close relationship between the mission of the Son and the pouring out of the Holy Spirit, and the joint celebration of the sacraments by which the Son and the Spirit come with the Father upon those who are baptized*" [34].[15]

The theological point made here is of such consequence that one feels compelled to wonder why it can be construed as applying only to adults and children of catechetical age [46] but not to infants and younger children, especially if these are baptized at the Easter Vigil. Unless the theological point is dismissed as mere rhetoric, it seems inescapable that all who are deemed fit for baptism, no matter what their chronological age, should also be confirmed within the same liturgical event. This seems in fact to have been the discipline in the Roman Church until the early Middle Ages, and it is still the practice of the Orthodox Churches, as we have seen. The continued practice of deferring confirmation of infants and children even into adolescence or early adulthood will have to take account of the theological principle stated clearly in [34]—a thing that would make the *age* of the candidate a serious obstacle to sacramental reception. But if this is the case, then it is inevitable that the same question be posed about baptism of infants. If age is a serious obstacle to receiving confirmation, why then is age not a serious obstacle to receiving baptism? Theological discussion will have to cope with this apparent anomaly.

While bishops, to whose office confirmation has been closely restricted in the Roman Rite, are urged to preside at the lenten catechumenal liturgies, to celebrate the rite of election, and to preside at the sacraments of initiation during the Easter Vigil [44], their necessary absence should not continue to force confirmation to be done quite apart from baptism and the eucharist. The document therefore opens the ministry of confirmation to any presbyter who has some diocesan function or office, who is a pastor either of the place where confirmation is celebrated or of any of the candidates, who has some catechetical relationship with the candidates, or who does the baptism itself.[16] Not only does this affect the traditional episcopal hegemony regarding confirmation in the Roman Rite, but it makes practicable a close connection between it and the other two sacraments of initiation, baptism and the eucharist, according to the theological principle of [34] mentioned above. This is a large step toward restoring a more coherent initiatory sequence, and it should affect for the better pastoral practice and theological reflection on these three sacraments as united phases of initiation. Far from constituting a restriction on episcopal ministry, it enhances this ministry by emphasizing the real sacramental importance of the bishop as the one who normally should preside throughout the whole process. Formerly this ministry was exercised almost wholly in confirmation and apart from the rest of the sequence.

Another structural clarification touches the two anointings with chrism, the one immediately after baptism and the other in confirmation. Since two chrismations so closely conjoined appear cumbersome, the document omits the postbaptismal chrismation when confirmation is to follow directly [224]. This clarification of structure is not, however, accompanied by an enlargement of language such a change seems to require. By this is meant that the prayer to be said at the postbaptismal chrismation speaks of the meaning of the act in terms of the neophyte's being anointed "As Christ was anointed Priest, Prophet, and King," so that he or she may always live as a member of his Body, the Church [224]. The prayer said for the chrismation at confirmation speaks, instead, of the neophyte's being given the Holy Spirit and his sevenfold gifts [230]. Thus when confirmation is celebrated *apart from* baptism, the chrismation after baptism is christic and messianic in character: when it is celebrated *with* baptism, the chrismation is pneumatic and charismatic. It could be argued that in this particular case a structural peculiarity in the Roman Rite has been exchanged for a verbal anomaly.

The confirmation phase concludes with a greeting of the neophyte but, unhappily as it seems, not with the kiss of peace [231]. This may be due to the Roman

Rite's placing the kiss of peace later, just before communion. Yet one would think that the final phase of the whole baptismal liturgy, culminating as it does years of catechesis and many experiences preparatory to this moment, is the perfect place for the first exchange of Christian peace between the presiding minister and the neophytes—and perhaps from them extending to the whole congregation. It would be a valid development were the emotional demands of so intense a sacramental moment to give rise to the solemn exchange of peace at this point, just as the first eucharist of Easter is about to begin.

A fourth and final matter deserves comment since it arises out of the preceding remarks. Unlike the old rubrics, which were restrictive on the minister to the point of moral and legal sanctions, these rubrics are elastic, expansive, and leave avenues toward further development open in light of future pastoral experience in the use of the rite. In addition, the rite provides a host of options for use by ministers, who will certainly find themselves in situations that demand liturgical adaptations to varying cultures and circumstances. This is simply liturgical good sense. The forms given are not restrictive but *normative*. As such they presume that local specifications of the general norm both will and must be made. Yet these specific local norms will still be able to recognize one another, for their common parent will be the same—this *Ordo Initiationis Christianae Adultorum* of 1972. If episcopal conferences and individual bishops allow informed and normal liturgical evolution to begin in the manner wisely forseen in the document, and if the celebration of its rites as valid outcomes of a renewed catechumenal discipline is responsibly done in local churches, the result cannot be other than a more catholic Roman initiation polity. And because the Church is constantly coming into existence through conversion and sacramental initiation, the result cannot also be other than a more effective and catholic Roman Catholicism. This last result will inevitably be of enormous ecumenical importance for the future.

PERIOD OF POSTBAPTISMAL CATECHESIS OR MYSTAGOGIA [37-40]

It is clear that conversion does not end with the sacraments of initiation. Rather, conversion in Christ among his holy people becomes the public possession of the whole local church each time initiation is brought to term in its premier sacramental phase. Because of this the Christian community more easily becomes a continuously converting people as it has regular access to the experience of individuals who move through the final stages of initiation each year.

The document makes it equally clear, however, that initiation does not end with baptism, confirmation, and first eucharist at Easter. If the entire initiation sequence from pre-evangelization through first eucharist has been well calibrated, the physical and emotional impact of the sacraments of initiation celebrated in the early hours of Easter morning should throw open a new dimension of the neophyte's consciousness that would permit deeper levels of faith to be articulated—levels that would have been, literally, inexpressible beforehand. If the catechumenal instructions have been more along the lines of Christian ethic and of how to live a Christian life—instruction typified by a practical concreteness that was at the same time suffused with a realistic and reticent reverence concerning the deeper mysteries of faith—the postbaptismal instructions can be more frankly theological and splendid in their scope.

It is not easy to be clear about this distinction between the character of prebaptismal and postbaptismal instruction. An illustration of it may, however, be detected by contrasting the ethos of the prebaptismal instructions sketched in the first six chapters of the *Didache* with that of the postbaptismal homilies of such later fathers as Ambrose of Milan, Cyril of Jerusalem, and John Chrysostom. These fathers rise to lyric heights in describing the mysteries into which the neophytes had only recently been baptized.[17] Chrysostom, for example, counts the "honors of baptism" in a sermon to the neophytes that fairly shimmers with cosmic symbolism in comparing the baptized to the fire by which the stars burn: "You are not only free, but also holy; not only holy, but also just; not only just, but also sons; not only sons, but also heirs; not only heirs, but also brothers of Christ; not only brothers of Christ, but also joint heirs; not only joint heirs, but also members; not only members, but also the temple; not only the temple, but also instruments of the Spirit. Blessed be God, who alone does wonderful things!"[18] Comparing the fathers' prebaptismal instructions with those given after baptism during the period of the *mystagogia* clearly shows the contrasts of style, tenor, and content that set the two forms of instruction off from each other.[19]

The rationale underlying postbaptismal catechesis or *mystagogia* should be seen not as having to do with some sort of *disciplina arcani*, but with the pedagogical fact that it is next to impossible to discourse effectively about an experience of great moment and intensity with someone who has never really had such an experience. One cannot speak tellingly of love to the unloving. Those who do love, moreover, speak not in analytical or discursive terms but in the language of poetry, music, and symbol. While the period of postbaptismal *mystagogia* is an ancient Church structure, its *raison d'être* is as valid as it ever was, given the document's view of conversion climaxing in sacramental initiation. The archaic is not the obsolete.[20]

Thus the document specifies that the main Sunday Masses of the Easter season should contain not only homiletic instructions for the neophytes and the whole local church: these Masses should also provide that the newly baptized retain their special places in the church [236], and that the readings for these Sundays may always be those contained in the new lectionary for year A.[21] What is expected to happen during this period is that both the community and the neophytes "move forward together, meditating on the Gospel, sharing in the eucharist, performing the works of charity. In this way they understand the paschal mystery more fully and bring it into their lives more and more. The period of postbaptismal catechesis or mystagogia is the final period of initiation of the newly baptized" [37].

To close the period of postbaptismal catechesis, around Pentecost Sunday, it is suggested that some form of celebration for the neophytes be held. The same is recommended for the anniversary of their baptism. Furthermore, the bishop is urged to "make sure, especially if he cannot preside at the sacraments of initiation, that at least once a year he meets the newly baptized and presides at a celebration of the eucharist" [239].

OBSERVATIONS

If the law of worship indeed constitutes the law of belief, and if the Christian initiation of adults is supreme among the Roman initiatory rites as the norm of them all, then all the local churches that make up the Roman communion need to take several matters most seriously.

For one thing, the document is clear and specific on who an initiated Christian is expected to be. He or she is not merely a set of abstract yet inexpressible good intentions that are thus incommunicable and subjectively sovereign. Rather, a Christian is a person of faith in Jesus Christ dead and risen among his faithful people. This faith is no mere noetic thing but a way of living together: it is the bond which establishes that reciprocal mutuality of relationships we call communion; it is this communion which constitutes the ecclesial real presence of Jesus Christ in the world by grace and character, faith, hope, and charity. This is what the eucharist signifies, celebrates, and causes within the community of the Faithful: it is the Church. This is what initiation in the fullest sense disciplines one for: it is the Church.

All other sacraments and sacramentals—from matrimony to holy orders to penance, anointing of the sick, vows and blessings—find their meaning and purpose only within this "economic" context. All a Christian's rights, privileges, and duties originate here. Here the Church's mission is constantly being set at the most fundamental level. Here the obligations to service and the limits on power and authority are established for all ministries within the Church, ordained or not. Initiation defines simultaneously both the Christian and the Church, and the definition is unsubordinated to any other except the gospel itself, no matter from what source other definitions may originate. This being the case, theological discourse, canonical reform, religious education, ministerial training programs and even the practical day-to-day running of dioceses and parishes will find it impossible not to take the present document as their starting point, for what it contains is not merely some more ceremonial changes for use *ad libitum*. Its core is an ecclesiology of rich existential concreteness and disciplinary clarity arising out of the best that two thousand years of Christian tradition has to offer.

The profound traditionalism of the document is sure to be interpreted by some as antiquarianism. While there are perhaps some instances of antiquarianism in the document, use of the provided rites will soon reveal what these are: then they can be either recast or dropped. But their presence should not blind one to the fact that what is old may also be truly traditional (there is no such thing as a "new tradition"). Understood correctly, tradition is a word denoting those aspects of a group's social compact which have managed to survive the traumas of history *because they work in maintaining the social group as a whole*. It is by this compact that the group coheres and is thus able to survive. Because of this, the social compact—however it is stated or left unstated—is the result of the entire group and its deliberative processes. Responsibility lies with the group itself and cannot be appealed to anyone's private "revelation," nor ought it to be taken from the group and handed over to anyone less than the total body politic.[22]

In an ecclesial sense tradition constitutes the summary consensus of the Church's total body politic, past as well as present, on points of the most crucial concern to the entire group. Thus differing from mere custom and convention, tradition frees from the tyranny of the present: it also protects against aggression by the compulsively articulate, as well as against opportunism by unchecked authority. The *Rite of Christian Initiation of Adults* represents that aspect of the social compact of the total body politic of the Church on the matter of who a Christian is and what, therefore, communities of Christians ought to be. As such, the document amounts to a sort of theological bill of rights for the whole of the Church's membership. It is meant to be not only read and understood but enacted regularly in sacramental deeds that cause what they contain. *Sacramenta significando efficiunt gratiam*: sacraments cause the grace they signify.[23]

If one factors into this theological focal point the main alterations in initiatory polity contained in the document, it becomes obvious how truly radical a renewal of Church life may result. The main alterations are these: *First*, the initiation of adults is regarded as the normal practice. *Second*, a catechumenate of serious content and duration is made again a standard Church structure. *Third*, the ministry of confirmation is opened up to presbyters in a good many circumstances. *Fourth*, the reason for this is to secure a close proximity of confirmation to baptism within the same liturgical event. *Fifth*, the document insists that there is, in addition, a most serious theological and sacramental set of reasons for this closer connection: It "signifies the unity of the paschal mystery, the close relationship between the mission of the Son and the pouring out of the Holy Spirit, and the joint celebration of the sacraments by which the Son and the Spirit come with the Father upon those who are baptized" [34]. *Sixth*, the immediately postbaptismal chrismation is omitted when confirmation is to follow, a reform that cannot help but enhance the pneumatic element in sacramental initiation. And *seventh*, prebaptismal and postbaptismal modes of catechesis are clearly distinguished.

NOTES

1. Typis Polyglottis Vaticanis, Vatican City 1972.

2. Para. 68-239.

3. Para. 240-277.

4. Para. 278-294.

5. Para 295-305.

6. Para. 306-369.

7. Included as an appendix in the Latin *typicum*, these rites are omitted from the English version of the United States

Catholic Conference and from the Pueblo Publishing Company's edition.

8. Para. 370-392. Paragraph numbers will henceforth be bracketed in the text.

9. Emphasis added for *Ecclesia, munere suo apostolico fungens*.

10. For precedents see J. A. Jungmann, *The Mass of the Roman Rite*, trans. F. X. Brunner (Benziger, New York 1950) vol. 1, 474-480.

11. See Balthasar Fischer, "Baptismal Exorcism in the Catholic Baptismal Rites after Vatican II," *Studia Liturgica* 10:1 (1974) 48-55.

12. See the vigil readings from the Old Testament: Genesis 1.1–2.2 (creation), Genesis 22.1-18 (Abraham's sacrifice of Isaac), Exodus 14.15–15.1 (the passage through the Red Sea), Isaiah 54.5-14 (God's mercy for Israel), Isaiah 55.1-11 (God's covenant), Baruch 3.9-15, 34 and 4.4 (the fountain of wisdom), Ezekiel 36.16-28 (pure water and a new heart).

13. *Apostolic Tradition* 21-22 (Whitaker 6).

14. Also para. 32.

15. Emphasis added for the even stronger words of the Latin: *Hac conexione significantur unitas mysterii paschalis, necessitudo inter missionem Filii et effusionem Spiritus Sancti coniunctioque sacramentorum, quibus utraque persona divina cum Patre baptizatis advenit.*

16. "When the bishop is absent, the presbyter who baptizes an adult or a child of catechetical age should also confer confirmation, unless this sacrament is to be given at another time [e.g., during the postbaptismal catechesis period or on Pentecost "in certain cases" (56)]. When there are very many to be confirmed, the minister of the sacrament of confirmation may associate other presbyters with himself in its administration" [46]. See also 228.

17. St. Ambrose, *On the Sacraments and On the Mysteries*, trans. by T. Thompson, ed. J. H. Srawley (SPCK, London 1966); *St. Cyril of Jerusalem's Lectures on the Christian Sacraments*, ed. F. L. Cross (SPCK, London 1966); *St. John*

Chrysostom: Baptismal Instructions, ed. P. W. Harkins, Ancient Christian Writers Series 31 (Westminster Publishing Co., Westminster, Maryland 1963). For an effective re-creation of the setting for the *mystagogia* in patristic times, see F. van der Meer, *Augustine the Bishop*, 347-387 and 453-467. For a thorough discussion of patristic mystagogy, see Hugh M. Riley, *Christian Initiation* (The Catholic University of America Press, Washington, D.C. 1974).

18. Quoted in *Baptism: Ancient Liturgies and Patristic Texts*, ed. A. Hamman (Alba House, Staten Island 1967) 166.

19. See, for example, Chrysostom's homily to the elect at the beginning of Lent and compare it with the one just quoted: Hamman, 139-151.

20. Victor Turner, "Passages, Margins, and Poverty: Religious Symbols of Communitas," *Worship* 46 (1972) 390-412 and 482-494, especially 391.

21. These same readings may also be used for the mystagogical period even when initiation is consummated at another time of the year [40].

22. Paul Ramsey raises the same issue in a civil context concerning the judiciary's "privatizing" the decision on who is to be regarded as human and thus possessing a valid claim to rights in American society: "Protecting the Unborn," *Commonweal* 100 (31 May 1974) 308-314.

23. Karl Rahner, *The Church and the Sacraments*, trans. W. J. O'Hara (Herder and Herder, New York 1963) 36. See the Council of Trent, session VII, canon 6 (*Enchiridion Symbolorum*, ed. Denzinger-Schönmetzer, [33]1965, no. 1606).

The Future

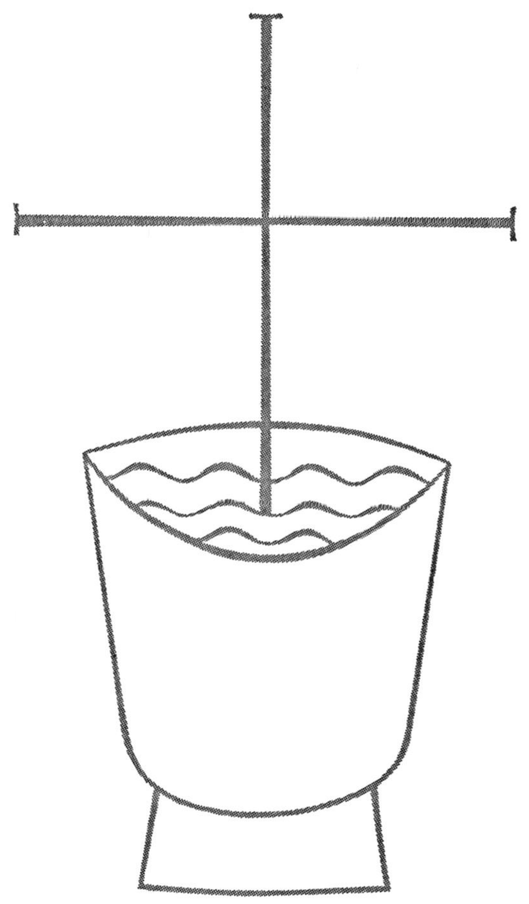

Chapter Six

Speculations, Observations, and Conclusions

If one studies the whole new Roman initiatory ensemble, particularly the *Rite of Christian Initiation of Adults*, there can be no doubt about its representing a polity that is quite specific with regard to who a Christian is. The ensemble sets before the Church of the present and future the image of a Christian as one who has attained a degree of maturity in faith that is manifested in a strong sense of Christian identity, both individual and corporate, through a considerable period of time in which belief in Jesus Christ has become a way of living together with others on a plurality of levels. This living together begins and ends as an act of worship of him from whom all good comes. It is a life of style suffused with a vigor which the world by itself cannot give. It lies only in the gift of God through Jesus Christ, a gift that cannot be merely received, but must be corresponded with, entered into, made one's own.

Christian tradition since biblical times has always risen from this concept as from an existential taproot. So fundamental has it always been to Christian reality that it has always escaped being reduced to a single mode of thought or enactment. For this reason the baptismal practice of Christianity has always been most flexible,[1] and plurality in baptismal usage is nothing less than apostolic in origin. In specific sacramental terms, the only thing orthodox tradition in east and west has been able to agree on is that the water bath and anointing with hand-laying are joined as closely as possible, in whatever order, in a compound act leading to the eucharist.[2] The major reasons for traditional plurality and flexibility seem to be twofold.

THE PASTORAL SENSITIVITY OF BAPTISM

First, the structures and rites for becoming a Christian lie on the turbulent leading edge of the Church's mission of ministry in the world. "Go therefore and make disciples of all nations, baptizing them in the name of the Father and of the Son and of the Holy Spirit, teaching them to observe all that I have commanded you; and lo, I am with you always, to the close of the age" (Matthew 28.19-20). So condensed and apodictic a summary of the Lord's own teaching has traditionally been found hard to ignore by the Church. Its initiatory polity in general and its initiatory structures and rites in specific will be found to be the most sensitive of all regarding the state of the world at whatever time the Church addresses it in fulfillment of its mission.

That the Church begins to change in response to a changing world first in its initiatory polity, its structures and rites, can be affirmed in its shift from a semitic to a hellenistic milieu; in its shift from being an illicit religion prior to the fourth century (the period of Tertullian and Hippolytus in particular) to being the religion of empire and culture in the fifth; in its shift from this to being tutor of civilization for teutonic and slavic barbarians after the sixth century and author of modern Europe and western civilization as we have known it. This last period was that of Christendom, an arrangement based on the close correlation of Church and State in an earthly City of God. Although the address of Church to world in the Christendom mold has been dissolving at least since the renaissance and seems to be reaching a terminal stage in our own days, the initiatory polity which evolved within Christendom was that which governed initiatory structures and ritual enactment until the Second Vatican Council was summoned by Pope John XXIII in 1959. While the polity was changed by the Council, and initiatory structures and rites have been brought into initial conformity with it, as we have seen in the preceding chapter, the attitudes of most Roman Catholics regarding baptism remain largely based on the initiatory polity of preconciliar Christendom.

This polity has, however, been rendered problematic not by the reforms of the Council but by the moribund state of Christendom itself. When, for example, there was a certain real correlation between Church and civil State as in western Europe during the medieval period, then the Church could and did expect that evangelization and catechesis could be accomplished on many levels by the culture itself—a culture which the Church largely authored through its tutorial role for the barbarian peoples who came both to civilization and to Christianity almost in one and the same step. In such a situation the Church could direct its attention toward keeping the focal points of political and cultural power reasonably Christian in order that preaching and exhortation to a more devout practice of the faith *within* the Church might function freely. Medieval initiatory polity was thus directed not so much at conversion of those outside to the faith as at conversion of those within the Church to lives of greater piety and more intense devotion, as exhibited in the many religious orders and pious lay movements spawned during this era.

In this perspective one might suggest that the ancient catechumenate in preparation for sacramental initiation by baptism, confirmation, and eucharistic communion really never died out as cultures were Christianized. Rather, the catechumenate gradually migrated into monastic and religious houses, there to be transformed into the novitiate and, later, into a seminary education. The sacramental ends of these "catechumenal" entities shifted correspondingly from baptism, confirmation, and eucharistic communion to religious vows and ordination. As one in earlier centuries entered the Church by conversion, catechesis, and the sacraments of initiation, now one would be said to have "entered the Church" by vocation to the evangelical counsels and by religious vows or ordination.

This development would be hard to underestimate so far as its effects on subsequent pastoral endeavor are concerned. Not only did it occlude baptism and contribute to its increasing association with infancy. It also caused the ethos of baptism to "bleed" into priestly ordination, charging the latter with qualities that would have astonished the two most famous presbyteral figures of the early Church, Origen and the waspish Jerome, each of whom took his basic vocations as teacher and scholar-ascetic far more seriously than his ordination as presbyter. But more importantly, holy orders as a baptismal surrogate would eventually lead to the notion that ordination is an inalienable right for all Christians, a demand sometimes based on Paul's *baptismal* admonition in Galatians 3.27-29 that "there is neither male nor female; for you are all one in Christ Jesus," and often laced with the *political* inference that baptism creates a Christian proletariat while ordination endows one with "first-class citizenship" in the Church. The steep decline in numbers of candidates for religious orders and particularly of seminarians in the years since the Council suggests that this view of religious vows and holy orders as baptismal surrogates is becoming nearly as moribund as Christendom itself. Attempts to bolster such a view in order to get more priests and religious should thus be viewed as mistaken at best, dishonest at worst, and futile in any case. Such attempts represent a retrograde movement searching for a type of Church that is fast ceasing to exist, and they ignore the type of Church that is rapidly evolving in a post-Christendom world more similar to that of the second than of the fourteenth century.

The Church's mission of ministry to the world is changing. The sensitivity of its conventional initiatory polity, especially in its surrogate forms centering on religious life and ordination since the period of medieval Christendom, not only demonstrates this but suggests certain avenues that ought *not* to be taken. One of these consists in trying to maintain a baptismal aura around any Church structure other than baptism itself. To do this is to associate baptismal reality and its attendant piety with something less than the entire Christian faithful, to whom the gospel promises baptism along with the eucharist as the birthright of all and as the foundation upon which fidelity in Jesus Christ rests. Although baptism is at the core of the commonwealth of the Church, the tendency in a post-Christendom era to associate its ethos and aura still with ascetical and clerical elites in the Church cannot stem only from the impetus of past practice. If sacraments have to do with meaning, and thus involve certain kinds of meaning and knowledge (*sacramenta significando efficiunt gratiam*), then there must be something in the meaning of baptism and in its attendant kind of knowledge as distinct from but related to all other sacraments that impels one to shrink back from it, to attempt to tame it, to associate it in surrogate form with specific groups in the Church that are more easily controlled than the community at large. This raises the second reason for the traditional plurality and flexibility of baptismal practice. The reason has to do with the nature of baptism's peculiar knowledge.

THE MEANING AND KNOWLEDGE OF BAPTISM

If nothing else, the plurality and flexibility of baptismal practice among the historic churches suggest that the meaning and knowledge peculiar to baptism as to no other sacrament overflow even the most elaborated rites. The observance of Christian initiation, which may take several years, detailed in the *Gelasian Sacramentary* of the eighth century, or in the *Rite of Christian Initiation of Adults* of the twentieth, says no more or less about the meaning of baptism into Christ than does the primitive catechetical and liturgical order contained in the first seven chapters of the *Didache*. Each of these three rites bespeaks in the accents of different times and in the language of different cultural and ecclesiastical circumstances the same unique and radically unspeakable mystery. They wisely, therefore, emphasize words far less than rich and ambiguous gestures, images, and sensations. They assert rather than argue, proclaim rather than explain, engage rather than discourse. Their classroom is a river, pool, bath house, or tomb. Their language is asceticism, good works, exorcism, bathing and anointing and dining. Their purpose is gradually to ease one into the love of God for the world through Jesus Christ in his life-giving Spirit, and to do so after the manner in which the Son himself consummated the same divine mystery by death and resurrection. At this point the entire round of the year's sequence of seasons is called upon to help, and the life-thrust of the cosmos itself is invoked in risky images of sexual fertility and through the inscrutable terrors of the grave. The Christian stands deep in all this, naked, covered with nothing but water and oil as night turns into day and as the fast becomes the Mother of Feasts. This is more than just a saving from sin or a classroom syllabus: it is, as the eastern fathers saw clearly, the divinization of humankind concretely accomplished through the incarnate Son dying and rising still among his faithful ones. It is from within this worldview that doctrinal discourse arises to reenforce and refine the conversional and initiatory experience, thus entering into dialogue with it. The law of worship constitutes the law of belief.

The Catholic and Orthodox worldview remains implacably sacramental because it has remained radically incarnational. It is reserved if not hostile toward attempts to reduce it into a series of conceptual propositions. It baptizes a convert not upon the basis of the convert's having been intrigued by some Christian doctrines, attracted by the Christian stance on some moral issue, or pleased by the aesthetic of some ceremony. It baptizes in the conviction that the convert either has begun by the Holy Spirit to live in Christ already or shows a marked likelihood of coming to do so at some future point in the fullest and most explicit ecclesial way. Faith, in this view, is not theology as it is practiced in academe: it is a way of life in Christ among his holy ones. Nor are these holy ones a loose association of the tasteful, the genteel, or the well-informed who desire to follow some of the teachings of a dead and absent Master. They are nothing less than those who corporately are strengthened by grace to bear the weight of God's pleasure for the world first manifested in Israel and finally brought to term in the personal individuality of the incarnate Son. The Church is not a palm potted in academe or a psychoanalyst's office. It is a Tree of Life whose vast branches hold ensnared a living if bloody Lamb; whose taproot sinks deep into the rich and murky waters of creation itself. Who would live in Christ must learn to climb with muddy feet, for there is nothing conventional, neat, or altogether logical about a crucifixion or the Church. Conversion in Christ involves broken hearts more than changes of mind. Augustine, perhaps the most towering intellect of his day, was more moved to faith by the sight of the Church at worship and by the voice of a child singing than the confessional apologies of Ambrose or arguments against the Manichees.

Roman Catholicism's sustained fascination with eucharistic questions since at least the ninth century has tended to impose a rather more tidy sort of sacramental knowledge on all this, obscuring and to some extent repressing it. For to know Christ sacramentally only in terms of bread and wine is to know him only partially, in the dining room as host and guest. It is a valid enough knowledge, but its ultimate weakness when isolated is that it is perhaps too civil. It lends itself to being conflated by short-term systems of cultural etiquette, thus becoming brittle and soon rendered obsolete when cultural patterns change. It is a knowledge prone less to robustness than to a niceness that readily sentimentalizes the Lord as guest and often transforms him as host into an indulgent therapist of whatever lusts may momentarily be ours. It is an Apollonian sort of knowledge in danger of going either soft or rigid.

Two main forces among others have traditionally balanced this tendency and checked its spread. The first has been the attempt at keeping the notion of "eucharist-as-meal" in tension with a notion of "eucharist-as-sacrifice." The tension calls one to remember that however elegant the knowledge of the dining room may be, it begins in the soil, in the barnyard, in the slaughterhouse; amid the quiet violence of the garden, strangled cries, and fat spitting in the pan. Table manners depend on something's having been grabbed by the throat. A knowledge that ignores these dark and murderous human *gestes* is losing its grip on the human condition. Its elegance is thus pruned to mere science: it can never evolve into the wisdom (*sapientia*) Aristotle and the scholastics held to be more than just knowledge (*scientia*). Wisdom is a rigorous knowledge so intimate, thorough, and profound that it goes through concepts and beyond them into the realm of sense and affection. It *tastes* and *sees* that God is. It is not irrational, but more than rational. It is supremely human. Christian ascetics and saints have called it contemplation pure and simple.

The second force that has traditionally balanced and checked the spread of an attenuated eucharistic knowledge of Christ has been baptismal. Baptism's knowledge of Christ is not that of the dining room but of the bath house. It is not a mannered knowledge, for manners, etiquette, and artifice fall away with one's clothes. It is a knowledge of appalling candor, hearty and intimate, less intellectual than physical—as when lovers are said to "know" one another. It is more the inspired wisdom of Solomon's Song than of Paul's letter to the Romans. God speaks not only in logic but in the aroma and feel of oil and warm water on the skin, and these too possess their own sort of rigorous logic.

This distinctive knowledge is not awfully civil. It is rarely brittle, and when cultures change it abides. Profligates and mystics share it: converts and lovers learn it quickly. It is difficult to articulate in classrooms and offices. It is rather uncouth to bring it up around a dinner table, for a mannered situation cannot survive too much knowledge of too radical a kind. Thus the noble aunt in Oscar Wilde's *The Importance of Being Earnest*, on being informed of her two grown nephews' approaching baptism, objects that such a thing must be regarded as grotesque and irreligious. That a bath house Christ leaves those grown accustomed only to a dining room Christ uncomfortable is precisely what it should do. His presence in the flesh had the same unsettling effect on his contemporaries. A robust baptismal polity and its attendant piety should secure that same salutary *contretemps* for his Body, the Church, in all ages. He comes to re-create by laying waste our conventional certainties, undercutting our limitations in order to free us to pass through them and come out on their other side—as he himself passed through death into a life no one had ever lived before. In his resurrection he did not return to life: he broke through it into a state that transcends life as we know it, a life made ours through the sacramental mysteries of the Church, his Body and the locale of his life-giving Spirit. This life is as different from the life we know as God's fatherhood is different from all human parenthood. To live in Christ is thus not like living in ordinary human society, as the disturbing events of Pentecost in the closed room made clear (Acts 2).

The knowledge peculiar to baptism is therefore implacably paschal.[3] As such it intimidates because it raises the inherent scandal and improbability of Jesus' death, resurrection, and outpouring of Spirit to a level of fundamental and rigorous "logic" upon which all Christian life, individual as well as corporate, must be based. The whole economy of *becoming* a Christian, from conversion and catechesis through the eucharist, is thus the fundamental paradigm for *remaining* a Christian. The experience of baptism in all its paschal dimension, together with the vivid memory of it in individuals and the sustained *anamnesis* of it in every sacramental event enacted by the community at large, constitute not only the touchstone of Catholic orthodoxy but the starting point for all catechesis, pastoral endeavor, missionary effort, and liturgical celebration in the Church. The paschal mystery of Jesus Christ dying and rising *still* among his faithful ones at Easter in baptism is what gives the Church its radical cohesion and mission, putting it at the center of a world made new. That world is a paschal world, and baptism in its fullness is the compound process of act and reflection by which one enters such a world, leaving behind an obsolete world where death is lord. The latter world was made by us all. The former is meant and made by God no less for all.

PASTORAL OBSERVATIONS

The Rite of Christian Initiation of Adults, in order to become more than a static curiosity in the Church's repertoire of rites or an ideal rarely if ever attained in practice, must be seen against this background as the refurbished manner in which all in the Roman Rite are expected normally to come to and sustain ecclesial faith. This prompts several sets of observations on the reformed rites from a pastoral viewpoint. These observations are undertaken in the knowledge that they will be neither exhaustive nor surrogate for actual pastoral experience in doing the rites over a considerable span of time. The acid test of any liturgy is always the degree to which its contents and ceremonial dispositions are in fact appropriated by those who use them.

In this regard all the reformed liturgical rites issuing from the Second Vatican Council present problems unique in the history of ritual evolution. For while change is a constant factor in all ritual systems, Christian or otherwise, the mode, quantity, and pace of ritual change since the Council is unique to the twentieth century and to the western churches. Previous to this century all ritual change occurred as an integral part of that long and slow development which was spurred by the gradual interplay between symbolic forms and the cultural idioms and rhythms with which they came in contact. In this process both symbolic forms and cultural idioms and rhythms changed more or less imperceptibly, modulating into a symbiotic relationship which over a long period of time kept the inhabitants of the culture involved in the process itself. Eventually, the process resulted in the emergence of a new cultural experience distinctively different from what had gone before and from all others that may have surrounded it. The cultural history of any human group is the story of this process.

It can be argued that the liturgical changes set in motion by the Second Vatican Council have indeed striven to do this by a policy not of introducing novelty but of reforming what was already of the tradition, thus striving to revitalize rather than to break continuity with the past. The argument is both true and false—true in strategic policy, false in the effects that policy has had on many Roman Catholics, both lay and clerical, in its rapid pace and in the great quantity of the reforms produced in slightly more than a decade. What has so far been accomplished is, in brief, a rather thorough revision of the Roman Rite's library of liturgical books, but even this has not yet reached a definitive form. It may not be too much to suggest that what the Roman Rite possesses at this stage is really all that committees can give, namely, an initial first draft of liturgical *reform* which will not be complete until the Church has had time to produce subsequent and more definitive drafts that can arise only out of extensive use of the reformed library in a host of pastoral situations. This experience will not only allow the Faithful time and opportunity to make the reformed rites their own: it will also inevitably demonstrate inadequacies in the present reform draft both as to structure and language, leading to refinements of the reform for years to come.

The most important symptom of the extent to which the reformed rites are in fact being appropriated by the Church at large, as well as the most important criterion for judging the quality of the refinement process, will be the degree in which liturgical *reform* leads to a qualitative *renewal* throughout the whole of Church life. The quality of Christian liturgy is always determined less by its conformity to past or present than by the extent to which it overflows itself, molding and enlivening the shared identity of its participants according to the criteria of the gospel of Jesus Christ. Baptism does not exist to generate doctrine but faithful Christians. The eucharist is not celebrated to consecrate hosts for communion or Benediction but to constitute and sustain the Body of Christ which is the Church. Good liturgy is so named not because it is a work helpful to the Church, but because it is nothing more nor less than the Church being most faithfully itself. In this, content and form are important, but neither is an end in itself. Each is a function of faith in practice, rather as the content and form of a language are functions of the world of meaning its speakers share—and in the sharing manage to cohere and thus survive. In this sense, a liturgy is the language a particular Christian faith-idiom speaks. Its quality is determined not merely by how and to what extent its content is re-formed, but more crucially by the extent to which it is constantly renewing, reenforcing, and reintegrating the faith community which uses it for survival's sake. An *unrenewing* liturgy, no matter how extensively it may be re-formed, betokens a church that is either dissolving, or moribund, or both. Renewal is the final criterion for judging the quality and appropriateness of liturgical reform.

No liturgical structure in the Church has more to do with the sustained renewal of Church life than its initiatory structure. Here, its new members are reformed according to the criteria of the gospel. The fresh appropriation in them of gospel faith as a way of thought and life on all levels renews not only them but the Church which initiates them into itself. In its catechumens and neophytes the Church local and universal has regular access in the most personal and concrete way imaginable to the renewing power of God's mercy in Jesus Christ. No convert ever believes in exactly the same way as any other. From this source the Church is constantly in receipt of the varied richness that is the most vital aspect of a faith claiming to be catholic.

The interim character of the reformed initiatory rites for adults, therefore, together with their potentiality for renewing the whole of Church life and practice, are the main factors underlying the following pastoral observations.

The Catechumenate

The first thing that strikes one about the document's treatment of the catechumenate is that "The rite of becoming a catechumen is of very great importance."[4] Further, the rite and the structure into which it introduces one presuppose a preceding period of "precatechumenate," said also to be of great importance and thus ordinarily not to be omitted.[5]

It is a time of evangelization during which the gospel of Jesus Christ is set firmly before the inquirer or "sympathizer" in an imperative way as the whole basis upon which the convert's sound intention to come to ecclesial faith is tested. If the *catechumenate* deals with ecclesial faith and how it is to be lived, the *precatechumenate* probes and renders stable the intention to come to that faith in the catechumenate.

Not only is this distinction pastorally essential in distinguishing different degrees of approach to the faith as lived: it also implies that requirements for *admission to the catechumenate* are in fact more stringent for adults than have usually been expected in recent years of those coming to baptism. Candidates for admission to the catechumenate "are required to be grounded in the basic fundamentals of the spiritual life and Christian teaching," to have already experienced initial faith and conversion of life, and to have already begun to repent and pray.[6]

In all this there is no hint that the several catechetical stages prior to sacramental initiation—precatechumenate, catechumenate, and purification or enlightenment—are anything but distinct levels of preparation that require both pastoral discernment and a certain sophistication in formation procedure. The process is discriminating not for elitist motives but out of concern for the convert and respect for the Church. Nothing can more readily turn into a caricature of itself than a religious conversion misdiagnosed or bereft of nurture and counsel. The responsibility of a local church to the converts its own well-lived faith attracts is second only to its responsibility to the gospel itself: the former is, in fact, only a dimension of the latter.[7] The catechumenate exists to temper Christian hospitality with a candid pastoral vigilance that is due both convert and Church in justice to each. The scrutinies give public form to this vigilance which has typified each stage of the formation process preceding the period of purification and enlightenment. The scrutinies will be empty formalities unless they rest on this foundation and are done in this spirit.

The same holds true for the catechumenal exorcisms and for the public dismissal of catechumens after the homily during the Sunday eucharist. Nowhere in the repertoire of the Church's public worship does an exorcistic structure exist so accessibly as in the liturgical scrutinies of the elect during Lent. The texts have been purged of too morbid a concern with demons, but the frank acknowledgment of the towering capacity of evil and its agents to maim even the best of human intentions remains. These texts articulate and give an admirable homiletic challenge to the Church to return to its humble dependence upon the power of God alone in Christ who saves, strengthens, and pardons. Our own strength remains insufficient: indeed, it is more often the problem than the solution. If nothing else, the catechumenal exorcisms are an instance of the Church's candor about what it cannot do. The same may be said of the catechumens' dismissal from the assembly of the Faithful before the eucharist proper begins. The catechumens' right is to the liturgy of the Word,[8] not to the eucharist. The latter comes only with the baptismal consecration which admits one to the order of the Faithful—those who, dead and risen in Christ and impregnated with his Spirit, possess the power to celebrate the sacrament of his Body and Blood in the communion of his Body, the Church. The regular experience of seeing those Christians not yet of the Faithful dismissed from the assembly after the service of the Word in a friendly yet firm manner and with prayer can, if well done, become a powerful catechesis of the Faithful themselves on the sublimity of their own baptism. This constitutes by itself a most valuable ministry rendered the Church at large by its catechumens.

The reinstitution of the catechumenate according to the directions given in the document must inevitably elicit a larger and more diversified corps of catechists than we have been accustomed to in the past. What must be done for catechumens is so multiform and extensive that no one person, no matter how well trained, can accomplish it all. The whole local community bears ultimate responsibility and must be summoned to the task of evangelization by faith and good example, of catechesis by witness in prayer and good works, of instruction in doctrine and Christian life, of joy in celebration, of repentance in justice and patience. If there are no converts, then the local church is failing in its evangelical task. If catechumens are rushed into sacramental initiation lest they languish and drift away, then the community is failing in all else. Catechumens should not ask for baptism in spite of the Church, but because of it. The state of the catechumenate will inevitably tell one much about the quality of the local church's corporate faith in Jesus Christ. If there is really little or nothing into which catechumens can be initiated, it would be better for the local church not to have a catechumenate. The problem is in a sense self-solving, for such a church will not be vigorous enough to generate much evangelical appeal in the first place. The circle is as closed as it is fatal.

To begin a catechumenate is a fateful step, and thus an intimidating one for many. It is to set changes in motion on every level throughout the parish and to expose the real health in faith of the local church for all to see. It is for a local church to put itself into the hands of the gospel and Christ's Spirit rather than under the safer and more manageable tutelage of conventions and programs. Nor should it be undertaken without fear, trembling, and a certain circumspection—but these, we are told, are the beginning of wisdom. They are, in addition, the overtures to changing a pastoral equation which, so long as it remains axiomatic, continues to produce results that block renewal even while it goes through the motions of reform.

Finally, it should be noted that there is no dearth of "catechumenates" either in the Church or civil society. None of these, unfortunately, currently exists in *direct* touch with the Church's baptismal structures. If one thinks of novitiates, these lead to religious vows rather than baptism. If one thinks of seminaries, these lead to ordination. Confraternity of Christian Doctrine programs often lead to penance and first communion, or to confirmation, or to none of these; but they rarely lead to baptism. Parochial school courses may sometimes be used in the same way, but their main concern is to educate for initiation into civil society at large rather than to aim for initiation into the Church by baptism. If one thinks of therapy groups such as Alcoholics Anonymous, these do an often successful job in shifting a "convert" from one pattern of life fraught with personal and social peril to another pattern of life more benign on both counts. In this, it provides many striking parallels with the early catechumenate, especially in its use of sponsors, its rigorous demands, and the intensity it generates in weaning one away from a destructive lifestyle by incorporating one into a social group that lives in diametric opposition to what went before. The same may be said in a more religious context of charismatic prayer groups, which do have a Christian initiatory thrust. But here the therapeutic end is less water baptism than "Spirit baptism" and its attendant manifestations of healing and glossolalia. The regularity with which this form of therapeutic "catechumenate" ends by initiating its converts into the mainstream of mature Catholic church life, especially on the local level, rather than into standard forms of enthusiastic sectarianism has yet to be seen. In the meantime, its stress on shared prayer and the consequent forming of the emotions and affections into a powerful social bond deserve careful study on the part of those who would embark on reinstituting a baptismal catechumenate as envisaged in the Roman document. One might say the same concerning other therapeutic entities in the modern Church, such as the Christian Family Movement, marriage encounter groups, Cursillo programs, and the like.

It is simply not true that if one would reinstitute the baptismal catechumenate one must start without helpful precedents and analogues for study. Such precedents exist in the tradition of the Church, as we have seen, and contemporary analogues abound. Yet it would be a mistake to think that any or all of these should determine what a restored baptismal catechumenate must be. A baptismal catechumenate is not merely a therapy group whose purpose is to instill enthusiasm in its members or render them better adjusted to live happily in Church or civil society. Such groups must not control the catechumenate: it must finally control them. It purveys not social or psychic well-adjustment, but the paschal mystery of Jesus Christ as a communal way of life, with all its passions, alienations, joys, and critical stresses. It should form people of sufficient strength in grace to live corporately a life that more often than not stands in radical opposition to the most cherished conventions of secular existence. In such a life poverty is neither something to be stamped out nor romanticized, but cherished for the gospel's sake; illness is seen to be as often a way to God as not; death is spoken of in the past tense, and life is all that lies in a future fraught with risks. Sin exists and evil squirms in every human heart. To deny these facts is to lead to a fantasy of the most disastrous sort for the Church as the pivot upon which creation turns. A candidate for Christian baptism must be brought not only to God's love but to a mistrust of cheap eschatologies and into vital opposition to empty presents—to a level of Christian maturity that can see triumph in the cross of Christ rather than poignant tragedy.

If the catechumenate develops the degree of gospel power it must in order to produce candidates of this sort for sacramental initiation, then those sacraments will inevitably have to recover a symbolic vigor commensurate with it. Sacraments are symbolic signs that *result* from contexts of meaning before and because of which they *enable* new dimensions of meaning to be discovered in and beyond their proper contexts. Since God's grace pervades the whole process, sacraments not only cause grace but are caused by it. If a given sacrament's result is detected as less than it ought to be, the trouble most frequently lies not in the quality of the liturgical act by which the sacrament is celebrated but in the diminution of the context of meaning out of which the liturgical enactment of the sacrament arises. The eucharist, for example, will not cause its full result (in scholastic terms its *res*, which is the unity of the ecclesial Body of Christ) if it is celebrated by a Christian community whose corporate life is uneucharistic before the sacrament is celebrated. To perform such an act results at least in a diminished sacramental effect which stands as a judgment upon those who do it.

There is nothing mechanical about sacraments. They do not trap God, but they may well convict of tempting him those who bring to them little or no meaning commensurate with their content. Baptism done anonymously and indiscriminately in a *pro forma* manner with little inconvenience to anyone, with drops of water and dabs of oil, is not merely a regrettable lapse in pastoral taste. It symbolizes and inevitably reenforces a view of the Christian mystery that is vastly at odds with everything the Church knows about the intent of its Lord. When this sort of baptism becomes the initiatory *norm*, the Church of Jesus Christ cannot repair the damage done its faith and ministry simply by more education and tighter administrative controls. It must enrich its context of meaning with regard to those who come to its faith and bring others to it through the catechumenate. It must also renew its initiatory sacraments which mark the end toward which catechumenal formation leads, and which constitute the foundation upon which all subsequent ecclesial life in Christ rests. Catechumenal and liturgical renewals are, therefore, to be viewed less as parallel options, either of which may be chosen more or less at random, than as interwoven processes, each of which involves the other as way implies end and as end presupposes way.

One might begin a renewal of the sacraments of initiation commensurate with a restored catechumenate first by determining what these sacraments embrace as a whole. Fundamentally, these are less three separate sacraments juxtaposed than one single initiatory event done in three stages. Both Catholic and Orthodox tradition concerning this united initiatory event may be summarized in four statements centering upon the New Testament's emphasis on messianic and pneumatic "sealing" in Christian baptism.

First, a sealing in the Spirit is included at some point within the total initiatory event *at least* by the early third and perhaps during the course of the second century.

Second, this sealing occurs in direct, intimate, and inseparable relationship with the Spirit-filled event of water baptism. Water baptism with its sealing, together with the equally Spirit-filled table event of eucharistic thanksgiving and communion, constitute baptism in its fullness.

Third, the form the sealing takes is that of a handlaying with oil, or consignation with pneumatic or epicletic prayer.

Fourth, the meaning, form, and location of the sealing have nothing to do with the physical, intellectual, emotional, social, or even spiritual "age" of the initiate. The sealing has rather to do with the fact that the initiate is entering into a Spirit-filled *community* through the death and resurrection of Jesus Christ who has himself become the life-giving Spirit by which the community believes, celebrates, and lives. If the sealing can be said to confirm anything it is, so far as the roots of Greek and Latin traditions are concerned, the initiate's baptism. Only by extension can it be said to confirm the initiate personally. The Church itself is the source of initiation as well as its end. Initiation is the process, both formative and sacramental, by which that Spirit-filled Body incorporates members into itself. Degrees of belonging to it are real only antecedent to baptism: after baptism they do not exist except by force of penitential discipline or according to the due process of law.[9]

There is a certain adamantine quality about this traditional witness that remains embedded in the various liturgical idioms by which the tradition is enacted—from Hippolytus to the *Gelasian Sacramentary* and the *Rite of Christian Initiation of Adults*—and that takes precedence over short-term pastoral needs. The whole initiation procedure—before, after, and including the water event—is pneumatically charged. The Holy Spirit is not confined to one event, confirmation, nor should this event be allowed to float free from the sacramental initiatory sequence. For when the "sealing" is absent the sacramental intelligibility of the whole sequence either collapses or mutates into something different. Baptism becomes an initial exorcism of sin, penance becomes a catechumenate for first communion, and confirmation becomes a baptismal surrogate during which one personally confesses one's faith before the Church, finally receiving the Holy Spirit. Paragraph 34 of the Roman document, as we have seen, recognizes the crucial position of the "seal" *within* the initiatory sequence in such strong theological terms that its association with the initiation of adults and children of catechetical age, but not with infants, appears anomalous.

This factor, when seen in the context of tradition's witness concerning the unity of the initiatory sequence outlined above, compels one to the following conclusion. Whenever it is deemed advisable to initiate a Christian, regardless of age, that Christian should be initiated fully and completely by water baptism, the "sealing" of confirmation, and first eucharistic communion. This should hold for everyone, although it may be found pastorally more advantageous to begin the sequence of baptism in its fullness so far as infants and very young children are concerned with solemn enrollment in the catechumenate followed by the sacraments of initiation in full sequence later at some appropriate time. To do this is *not* to "delay baptism." *It is to begin baptism in its fullness as soon after birth as practicable, and to celebrate its stages over a period of years according to the child's growth in faith*, rather than to telescope the sacraments of initiation into a few minutes or dismember the sacramental sequence altogether.

As radical as this change in conventional procedure may seem to many Roman Catholics, the notions of the catechumen's being already a Christian in a true degree of communion with Christ in his Church, of the intrinsic place of confirmation *within* the normal sequence of sacramental initiation, and of the inalienable rights that accrue to one baptized by water and the Holy Spirit, together make the change theologically respectable. One also suspects that the demands of Christian existence in a post-Christendom world will make the change pastorally inexorable. Indeed, it continues to be the normal polity of sacramental initiation in the Orthodox Churches to this day, a polity shared by the Roman Church until the early middle ages when the emergence of western Christendom seemed to render that polity increasingly redundant and finally obsolescent.

But theological respectability, pastoral inexorability, and historic precedent are not the only factors that should encourage the Church to yield to this shift in conventional procedure. More compelling even than these is the need for individuals and local churches to have the strongest possible sense of their own Catholic identity, an identity not rooted primarily in their ethnic past or even in the religious rhythms of family and school, *but an identity rooted in the living memory of their own baptism into Christ in his Church*. A Christian must have such a memory—whether it derives from regular participation in the baptism of others or, better, from one's own—as both a corrective and an enrichment for all his or her subsequent sacramental encounters. A memory of one's own ordination without a balancing memory of one's own baptism into the chosen race, the royal priesthood, the holy nation of God's people must often give rise to an overweening regard for holy orders at the expense of all else. A memory of one's own wedding without an enriching memory of one's baptism into the vast wonder of God's "marriage" to humanity in Christ must often enervate matrimony and imperil the family. Looking upon the dead face of one beloved without a memory of one's own definitive death to death in the waters of life must often give rise either to mute stoicism or morbid despair. What the eucharist remembers and actualizes as the great *anamnesis* of the Church is not primarily the Jesus of flesh and history but the Anointed One of pre-time, end-time, and paschal glory who can be known only in baptismal faith. The eucharist is thus most profoundly the constantly reiterated "seal" of baptism, as baptism is its unique and unrepeatable introit. *The eucharist, being the way baptism always comes to rest with Catholic Christians throughout their lives, is unavoidably the sacrament of Christian maturity*. For this reason it is the eucharist that ends the sequence of sacramental initiation, not confirmation.[10] Confirmation "seals" baptism in such a manner that thereafter the eucharist is not only a rite but a Spirit-filled way of corporate life in the Body of Christ which is the Church—a life all must live, a rite to which all must therefore have access irrespective of age.

The memory of all this, at once paschal and baptismal, is so fundamental to Christian existence and pastoral ministry that its enrichment at every point is of the utmost urgency. Minimalism in the sacraments of initiation constricts not only all the other sacraments but the whole of Church discipline and polity as well. Proliferation of minimalism—such as by hurriedly baptizing people, especially infants, at Sunday Mass without prolonging the usual time of the service so as to avoid traffic problems—is still minimalism, even more so if at the paschal vigil there do not happen to be any baptisms at all. Some rearrangement of Sunday schedules to accommodate adequate celebration of the sacraments of initiation in their fullness simply must be made, perhaps by taking the whole time of one scheduled Mass for baptism and confirmation, ending with a blessing and dismissal after the homily for those in the congregation who must leave (having thus truly fulfilled their obligation of Sunday worship); then taking the whole time of the following Mass for the first eucharist and communion of the neophytes, beginning with the prayer of the faithful. This is a makeshift plan cited here as an extreme example of how, failing all else and given the crucial importance of sacramental initiation, the Sunday schedule in busy parishes ought to give way rather than continue to force minimalism upon baptism in its fullness. More importantly, however, the *Rite of Christian Initiation of Adults* in its paragraphs 49-62 concerning the times of initiation implies that a whole repertoire of initiatory events—enrollments in the catechumenate, elections, scrutinies, and sacraments—will gradually have to be absorbed into the regular scheduling of Catholic liturgical services along with weekday and Sunday Masses, confessions, devotions, and celebrations of the liturgy of the hours. This also suggests that ministers, especially presbyters and bishops, will have to learn to preach in baptismal contexts in addition to eucharistic ones. The consequent raising and broadening of homiletic consciousness on the clergy's part will be welcome, no doubt, by all.

Finally, lest all this seem much ado about what might still remain liturgically very little, the symbolic elements involved in the sacraments of initiation will have to regain much of the robustness that has always been intrinsically theirs. Water and oil on the skin, the aroma of chrism, the taste of bread and wine (and perhaps even Hippolytus' milk mixed with honey), the sounds of songs and ovations, the sight of the assembly rejoicing, the touch of another's hands, a kiss of peace and welcome—all these elements should work in harmony. They give both the baptized and the Church baptizing its multidimensional, catholic, paschal and therefore irreducible orientation in Christ. In a culture trained largely by words and visual "messages" that try to develop intellectual conceptualization, it is even more crucial than it ever has been to give Christians more than concepts alone, important as these are. Christians individually and corporately also need access to a radical experience and sense of rightness; of standing at an axial spot from which everything radiates out and to which everything falls home; of dwelling splendidly at the center of things.[11] This experience and sense form the basic orientation that must undergird the whole of ecclesial life, going far beyond the audio-visual aids of the classroom or the devotional aids purveyed by ecclesiastical goods companies.

Basic orientation mobilizes that whole sense of where one stands toward one's need to survive in the present and future. It raises the organism to a peak of physical and psychic coordination where it "knows" to a degree never otherwise attainable. The dog "points" its game; the wrestler prepares to attack; the blind touch and thus "see"; the mystic moves from mere meditation into true contemplation; lovers exclude all else in their mutual gaze. The Church baptizes. The senses of touch, sight, smell, hearing, and taste lose their separateness to fuse into one state of perception. The eye penetrates the icon; smell ingests the environment and the body occupies it, tasting it on the tongue as the ears devour its sound. Perception fuses in space with time, and a thing is not just known but possessed with so indelible an intensity that it will never be forgotten. But it can never be put into words alone.[12]

No liturgical complex in the Church's repertoire is so capable of attaining this sort of power as that of sacramental initiation. If Christian identity both individual and corporate seems on the wane under contemporary pressures, it may be traceable in large part to the attenuation of the experience and sense of basic orientation in the Church's initiatory practice. The dignity of one's baptism needs more than drops of water, dabs of oil, taps on the cheek, and plasticized bread dipped in a modicum of wine. Baptism into Christ demands enough water to die in, oil so fragrant and in such quantity that it becomes the Easter aroma, kisses and *abrazos*, bread and wine enough to feed and rejoice hearts. And rooms of glory filled with life rather than crumpled vestments and stacks of folding chairs.

Immersing and anointing bodies can be done unashamedly without being indecorous, but these things cannot be done in fonts on wheels except for infants, and they should not always have to be done before the whole parish community. The baptistry must be used well for those events in which a certain decorum is appropriate. The sealing of baptism in confirmation should, however, be normally set amidst the whole community. In all things, the purpose must be to allow the power and vigor of those events which make a Christian to emerge from the constrictions that have hemmed them in for centuries. The end will not be the death of decency but the Church's rediscovery of itself as the glorious Body of Christ, damp with his blood and fragrant with his own anointing at his Father's hands. The experience and sense of this in the memory of every Christian is where renewal has always begun throughout the Church in all its members, for it is the point at which the Church is constantly being born.

PASTORAL CAUTIONS

One purpose of this book has been to recommend the *Rite of Christian Initiation of Adults* as a powerful stimulus to the renewal of Christian living in the Roman Catholic Church. Yet this very power, which is always present in any vigorous initiatory polity, leads to a need for certain cautions lest it mushroom out of control and rend the very fabric of communal living in faith the document is meant to presume and foster. These cautions can be grouped under the three main headings which follow.

Taming the Catechumenate

Of most serious concern is that the power implicit in a renewed initiatory polity such as contained in the *Rite of Christian Initiation of Adults* will lead some people to conclude that many if not all its specific features will have to be tamed drastically to fit contemporary Church life in twentieth century America. While modifications will surely be found necessary after a period of use, it would be a serious pastoral mistake to diagnose these in advance according to criteria that may often be contrary to the stated intent of the document or even inimical to the gospel itself.

To reduce, for example, the solemn enrollment of catechumens to an informal gesture of cheery hospitality toward inquirers that takes place at a parish party makes too little out of this serious step into the Church, trivializing if nothing else the evangelization that prepared for it and the incipient conversion that has so far taken place, usually with pain and at great cost, in the catechumens themselves. Yet [14] points out that this event is of "very great importance," and that it is nothing less than a function of the Church's "apostolic mission."[13] The same thing can happen to the scrutinies of the elect during Lent if they are constricted into benign routines for inculcating a shallow optimism about the liberality of grace, a rosy future of Christian living, or a notion of sin and evil as something that stems merely from human inadvertence. To do such a thing is not merely to misunderstand the document; it is to fall under the gospel's judgment.

Nor should the catechumenate regularly be confined into one year of largely doctrinal instruction made up of two tidy "semesters"—a winter one ending with Christmas and a spring one ending with "commencement" at Easter. Conversion, which is what catechesis is about most profoundly, is not so easily regimented. For some, several years may be needed for faith to mature in them to a point at which ecclesial election for baptism would become possible. The catechumenate is not, one must repeat, primarily a course in theology for lay people, nor is it a course in ethics based on current events. It is a structure for Christian nurture that must be carried out in multiform ways and with sustained and patient discernment over a considerable period of time. It is not identifiable with the sort of nurture needed by baptized penitents: even less is it the same as the nurture stemming from public sacramental worship and preaching appropriate to the Faithful. These differing modes of nurture, while related, remain distinct and must not be conflated lest they all be weakened.[14]

A similar caution ought to be exercised concerning the temptation to reduce the local church's role in forming, scrutinizing, electing, and baptizing catechumens down to a certain symbolic number of the Faithful who go through the whole of a brief "catechumenate" with the catechumens. The danger here lies not only in having catechumens overly influenced by certain of the Faithful whose piety is certifiable by obscure standards, or who possess ecclesiastical tastes, or are inebriated with religious enthusiasm of an elitist kind. The real danger lies in overlooking the matter for which the Church as a whole should have the most concern, namely, the formation of new members for initiation into itself—an act of which it is the main sacramental agent in and after Christ himself.[15] Catechumens are not baptized into the piety of their pastor or catechists, nor into the ebullience of the local charismatic prayer group. They are baptized into the Church, Christ's Body—faith, warts and all. This is a matter over which pastors and bishops should watch with greatest care lest Christian initiation produce people who are something either more or less than faithful members of such a Body.

Finally, a regular delaying of confirmation from Easter until Pentecost, during which interval the neophytes return to class sessions called "mystagogical," may strike some as educationally neat or charismatically appropriate; but its conformity to the document is merely extrinsic at best. More seriously, such procedure once again causes dislocation in sacramental sequence by separating confirmation from baptism and inserting holy communion between the two. It may privatize for the neophytes the period of mystagogy meant for the whole local church during the paschal season and reenforce a didactic view of catechesis. Catholic tradition has maintained Pentecost not as the special time for *confirmation* but as the next most appropriate time for *baptism in its fullness* after Easter itself.

In all these instances what one detects is no lack of good intentions, but rather an initial felt need to conform the restored initiatory polity to some of the very practices it was meant to change. As such, the *Rite of Christian Initiation of Adults* could imperceptibly come to be regarded not as a pastoral challenge but merely as the latest and most novel way for doing old things even worse, thus helping them better not to work. For if the fate of the catechumenate is to become nothing more than another educational program, it is difficult to see how true penitence for sin, apostolic involvement in works of mercy, and spiritual maturation under wise direction—all salient aspects of catechumenal nurture stressed in [19]—will be accomplished. It is simply not true that educational programs of themselves produce such things: as often as not they spawn ethical permissiveness by relativizing values, devotion to middle class affluence, and a certain spiritual hubris. Educational patterns and techniques as worked out in modern western culture are far more efficient initiators into that culture than into one specifically based on gospel values, as the inefficiency of parochial schools in transmitting Christian religious values demonstrates.

When the nurture and formation of catechumens for full ecclesial faith and its exercise are concerned, therefore, modern educational patterns and techniques should be used with caution.

More promisingly, the Roman document suggests that *other ways both exist and can be found* to accomplish this sort of nurture and formation. This means that in founding catechumenates one should look to a range of other structures for help—some of which have been already mentioned in this book.[16] It also means that the Church's own resources should be looked to. Examples of these are the Church's rich heritage of ascetical, mystical, and spiritual writings from the gospels to Paul, from Anthony of Egypt to Cassian, Benedict, John of the Cross, Teresa of Avila, Thomas More and Merton; its intrinsically robust sacramental and liturgical celebrations; the vast scope of its stunning record of charitable enterprise which tutored Europe and began the civilization of the New World. To allow all this to lie fallow in favor of succumbing to recent reductionisms, under the apprehension that these will assure the Church's relevance and efficiency today, will almost surely make the Church even more a part of the problem than it already is. But its mandate and vocation is to be in Christ the unique solution to the perennial problem of life and death, virtue and vice, freedom and slavery rather than one of its many parts. Nowhere does this issue come more crucially to the fore than in the process by which the Church takes new members into itself.

Distinguishing Ministerial Roles

The diversification of ministry in the Church is one of the most promising pastoral developments to have begun since the end of the Second Vatican Council. In a real sense this development was inaugurated by the insistence of the *Constitution on the Sacred Liturgy* upon the dignity and integrity of all roles of liturgical ministry—bishop, presbyter, deacon or layperson, celebrant, server, commentator, singer, reader or whatever. These ministerial roles are to be respected and kept distinct while acting in concert. They are not to be conflated or overridden by clerical impatience or malfeasance.[17]

This same principle applies with equal or even greater force to the process of catechumenal formation and sacramental initiation. As has been frequently noted here, this whole process is of such duration and complexity that no one person can minister to it all, even if one were to find an individual who possessed all the gifts necessary for such a ministry. Experienced teachers are not the only ones who are needed, nor is their special expertise either the main or the only one required in conversion therapy. A true catechist may indeed be a good teacher, but not every good teacher makes a true catechist. An ordained priest may be a good preacher or administrator, but ordination does not necessarily confer all the gifts needed for prudent discernment of intentions; nor does it make the ordained an automatic example of one who prays so well that a catechumen could be encouraged to pattern his or her prayer life on this person's example.

Nor should just anyone be chosen as sponsor or godparent.[18] Concerning these, the catechumen should choose his or her godparent as the catechumenate proceeds and as the catechumen's faith and perceptiveness deepen.[19] These godparents then become the most intimate examples of ecclesial living for the catechumen. They should attend at least some of the catechumenal sessions with their charges, become involved in its activities of prayer and witness and good works, and assume overt roles in the final scrutinies, anointings, and sacraments of initiation. But their role does not stop here. It should continue after initiation as main support for the neophyte at least until such time as the new *fidelis* is finally mature enough in faith to stand firmly on his or her own feet.

In all this the role of the ordained minister is mainly one of oversight, especially if he is a presbyter. As a rule, the parish priest's efforts should be directed at establishing the catechumenate, staffing it with the best persons representing a wide variety of gifts relative to conversion therapy and instruction, and overseeing its continuing function throughout the year. While he will preside at its more formal and public sessions with the more senior catechumens, he should probably not become too intimately involved in its ordinary running. He should trust his catechists, sponsors, and godparents since in many ways they are more competent to deal with the formation of converts—on initial levels especially—than he probably is. Too great or too early an influence on his part not only runs the risk of clericalizing catechumen, catechist, and the whole formation process. It may also place an unhealthy set of stresses on him, engross him too much, and thus warp the ministry which only he can render to other groups within the local church.

He needs, in particular, to maintain a real distance from the often searing demands any therapeutic process places on its participants. In conversion therapy the confrontation with evil working its ways upon people coming to faith is so special and demanding a matter that the Church in earlier centuries recognized a ministry mainly devoted to it. To exorcize was, like healing, regarded as a ministry the Church could not commit to people through the laying on of hands. It could only be acknowledged in persons who demonstrated the charisms for coping with evil whether in its spiritual or physical manifestations. These charisms come directly from the Holy Spirit, and they touch relatively few: they cannot be institutionalized, and they are very special indeed. An ordained person may possess them, but this is rare and in no way part of the regular gifts of ordination as such. One must not confuse sacraments and charisms but sustain a healthy respect for the latter when they appear. They are evidence of the Spirit's having blown where it will for the Church's good.

A priest who is naive about all this risks not only personal damage but also puts his church at risk in the warping of his ministry that may result. The presbyterate's main function is not to be all things at all times to all people. It is to provide wise counsel ("presbyter," after all, means "elder") to the whole Church by being above all else a man of the Church. A presbyter is not a prophet *per se* any more than he is an exorcist or a faith healer, an analyst or a social worker. As such, his ministry is as modest as it is crucial: it is to preach wisely and well, to oversee with a firm but circumspect prudence, to preside simply and without pretense at worship, to care deeply for his people, to judge justly in fear and trembling, and to respect and foster charisms in others for the building up of the Church. He is the main facilitator in the local church, not a living clot of surrogates for everything it must do for itself as the Body of Christ.

Nowhere, again, does this issue come more crucially to the fore than in the process by which the Church takes new members into itself. In this area above all a real diversification of ministry will be necessary. This means not acceding to pressure from special-interest groups to have their members "honored" by being commissioned as special ministers of communion or using the diaconate as a sort of ecclesiastical award. Restoration of the catechumenate means the Church will have to become even more serious about ministerial diversification. It must finally get over the notion that ordination is an accolade instead of an incorporation into *orders* of service to the Church, and through it to the world. For baptism is the fundamental act of sacerdotal incorporation in the Church, an act upon which all ordinations depend both for their meaning and validity. The Church baptizes to priesthood: it ordains to episcopacy, presbyterate, and diaconate.

Distinguishing Catechumens

A catechumen is one who is being prepared for sacramental initiation into the Church. In practice such persons will often be found to be of two main types: 1) those who have never been validly baptized, and 2) those who have been baptized but never confirmed or communicated—who, in other words, have never had their baptism fully sealed in ecclesial communion. The former are catechumens in the fullest sense since they are coming to ecclesial faith and sacramental initiation for the first time: they are the primary subjects of the Roman Rite's normative initiatory polity. All others are, without prejudice, secondary (e.g., those who have been baptized but not confirmed or communicated) or tertiary subjects of that polity (e.g., the already fully initiated Faithful who may be seeking spiritual growth or renewal in the catechumenate).

It seems necessary to keep clear the distinctions between these different sorts of persons lest the catechumenate lose its essential form and purpose to become a catch-all structure for parish educational needs outside the parochial school, or an extension program of the Confraternity of Christian Doctrine for adults. Neither of these two otherwise worthy enterprises is what a catechumenate is. Faith comes not by education but by the grace of conversion, and it is this last for which the catechumenate exists—to develop and deepen it to a point of ecclesial maturity that can be sacramentally sealed by baptism in its fullness.

In view of this, the *already initiated who seek spiritual growth or renewal in the catechumenate* should probably be kept out of it. What they seek is thoroughly admirable, but it is what should be particularly available to all in the Church during each lenten season if the parish's liturgical life, its preaching, and its apostolic endeavors are all they should be. Beyond these, more special parish programs such as retreats, quiet days, and prayer and study groups ought to be available for such persons. Above all there remains the penitential structure with its counsel, asceticism, and sacramental resolution—a structure admirably analogous to that of the catechumenate in its "period of enlightenment" during Lent. As catechumens are initiated at Easter, so also the penitents as a group might, after lenten prayer and fasting, be reconciled on Holy Thursday and communicated at the Mass of the Lord's Supper, or on Good Friday. The catechumenate should neither lose its distinctive nature nor cannibalize other structures. To use it as the sole parish spiritual renewal program would almost certainly swamp its specific concern for converts coming to faith within the Church for the first time. What the catechumenate is for these persons, Lent and penitential structures ought to be for the Faithful.

If, however, the never baptized are the fundamental concern of the catechumenate, and if those sincerely seeking spiritual renewal are the fundamental concern of other structures, the *only partially initiated* (i.e., the baptized but never confirmed or communicated) are a more complex matter. They are also apt to be more numerous in many places than the never baptized, and they thus present a special set of catechumenal problems. They may be persons whose baptism in infancy is quite unremembered and has never been functional in their lives: in this case they will have to be treated in ways closely similar to those employed in conversion therapy for the never baptized. Yet their baptism should never be ignored, and it must never be repeated.[20] This may mean that they should best be treated as catechumens in all things except that they are not dismissed from the eucharist with their unbaptized colleagues: but neither should they be communicated because their baptism has not yet been publicly confirmed with the seal of the Spirit, an act in which full communion in the Spirit-filled Church comes to ecclesial and sacramental consummation.

This policy has the advantage of being consistent with what ought to be done regarding the other main sort of only partially initiated catechumens. These are those whose baptism has been validly accomplished in another Christian communion, being a clearly remembered event that has been fairly functional in their lives even up to and through their request for reception into the Roman Catholic Church. Such persons may or may not have been, in addition, validly confirmed in the other communion. In any case, their maturity in faith, and the degree to which this faith approximates ecclesial explicitness, will have to be well diagnosed in order to determine to what extent they ought to be treated as catechumens in the full sense. It may well be that conversion therapy would be largely redundant, and that in reality only some doctrinal instruction and a period of familiarization with the local church and with Catholic tradition and piety would be necessary. No *a priori* rules can be given that would substitute for sound diagnosis of individual cases in matters such as this. But such persons should not be dismissed from Mass before the liturgy of the eucharist, nor should they be communicated until either their baptism is confirmed or, if this sacrament has already been validly received in another communion, they are received into full communion with the Roman Catholic Church according to some form appropriate to the individual case itself. Such forms need to be worked out that are congruent with a significantly changed ecumenical climate. Here too, nothing can subsitute for an informed pastoral sensitivity with regard to such delicate matters. Not every human circumstance can be foreseen by norms, and the Holy Spirit blows where it wills.

Yet one serious problem appears to exist concerning this matter in the document's normative dispositions for sacramental initiation and should be mentioned here. It involves what is to be done about the baptized but never confirmed in the celebration of sacramental initiation, in particular when this is celebrated at the paschal vigil. Chapter IV of the document [295-305] is devoted to the preparation of such people for confirmation and eucharist, all its stipulations being firmly based upon the paradigmatic way in which the never baptized are prepared for the sacraments of initiation.[21] Yet these *baptized catechumens*, even though they may well have gone through the whole catechumenal sequence with their colleagues, with the exception of their not being dismissed with the rest before the eucharist begins due to their baptism,[22] *by this same token are not to be confirmed if "the bishop or the extraordinary minister of the sacrament is not present."*[23]

This insistence on the presence of the *bishop* seems to imply that a presbyter who licitly baptizes and confirms unbaptized catechumens according to the stipulations of [46] cannot confirm an already baptized catechumen who has gone through the whole process with all the rest. Such a person would perforce be neither baptized nor confirmed during the service, but might well *be communicated* then and confirmed by the bishop only later and probably elsewhere. The resulting liturgical and pastoral situation this creates in the actual celebration of the sacraments of initiation involving the rest of the catechumens and the whole local church at the paschal vigil is most awkward and seems to be quite at odds not only with [34] but with [304] itself: "the climax of [the already baptized catechumens'] whole formation will normally be the Easter Vigil. Then these adults will profess their baptismal faith, receive the sacraments of confirmation and take part in the eucharist."[24] The *sacramental* awkwardness again consists in separating confirmation from baptism and inserting communion between the two. The *pastoral* awkwardness lies in how this baptized catechumen's *not* being confirmed with his or her colleagues is to be explained to the community celebrating their initiation into itself at the paschal vigil. The distinct possibility is that it will appear that some penalty attaches to the *baptized* catechumen which only the bishop can deal with.

Yet this awkwardness becomes an anomaly with the mention of an "extraordinary minister" being able, along with the bishop, to confirm an already baptized catechumen. Some may detect here an echo of canon 782, which defines the bishop as the "ordinary minister" of confirmation and then goes on to specify that the "extraordinary minister is a presbyter to whom either common law or a special indult from the Apostolic See concedes this faculty."[25] It must be remembered, however, that this canon has been rendered largely obsolete by [46], which in turn rests upon paragraphs 7 and 8 of the introduction to the new *Rite of Confirmation*. In paragraph 7 the technical definition of the bishop as the "ordinary minister" of confirmation has been deliberately changed to "original minister": *Confirmationis minister originarius est Episcopus*.

There then follows a list of those presbyters who can now confirm in the bishop's absence. In paragraph 8 the "extraordinary minister" of confirmation mentioned in canon 782 is added to this list.

Three matters deserve comment in view of the foregoing. First, while the bishop, due to his unique pastoral ministry in the Church, remains the premier minister of confirmation (as he is of the whole liturgy of Christian initiation), presbyters who are involved in the sacraments of initiation according to the stipulations of those paragraphs of the new Roman documents mentioned above now can confirm not by delegation but by law. When they do so, such presbyters act in a canonically "ordinary" manner, although the bishop remains the "original minister" of the sacrament and takes precedence whenever he is present. Second, paragraph 7b of the *Rite of Confirmation* states explicitly that such a presbyter can confirm an already baptized *adult* who is being received into full communion with the Church. Since the liturgical setting is specifically said to be that of a reception into full communion of one already "validly" baptized, the presumption seems to be that the persons referred to are not already baptized Roman Catholics but non-Roman Catholics. Third, [304] envisions a celebration of the sacraments of initiation at the Easter Vigil in which confirmation cannot be given due to the absence of the bishop or the "extraordinary minister"–that is, a normal initiatory event in which the presiding presbyter cannot confirm. What such an event might be is left to conjecture, but in light of paragraph 7b of the *Rite of Confirmation* it would appear that such an event might be one in which everyone *but* already baptized Roman Catholics and children validly baptized in another Christian communion would be confirmed by the presiding presbyter. The implication is that these persons will have to be confirmed by a bishop or "extraordinary minister." The reason for this is as obscure as it is unstated, leading one to suspect that some clarification will be needed if the sacramental and pastoral awkwardness mentioned previously is to be avoided.

THEOLOGICAL OBSERVATIONS

One must not romanticize the results that may flow from the restoration of a more vital sacramental practice of Christian initation in the Roman Catholic Church. As power-laden as these results can be, and as radical as they will be for every aspect of Catholic life, they not only face a certain pastoral inertia on the part of many in the Church but are in fact intimidating in their theological implications as well. It is better to be candid about some of the latter here.

First, the use of baptism in theological apologetics as a sign of God's complete gratuity in the giving of himself cannot serve as basis for a policy of indiscriminate baptism. Such a policy is simply at serious odds with the New Testament and traditional doctrine of justification by faith in Jesus Christ dead and risen in his Church. Baptism has always involved discernment and discrimination according to the demands of a gospel which perceives life in Christ as the result of one's having first entered fully into his passion and death. The reality of which Christian baptism in its fullness is sacramental symbol and efficacious sign is Jesus Christ's passage from death to life, from flesh to Spirit, from the limits of this world into the freedom of the kingdom of God. The Church which baptizes is not a garden club that putters around with good intentions: it is a threshing floor on which God works his tough but gracious will in the world after the pattern manifested in the life, death, and resurrection of his only Son. Under grace and in the Spirit, the Church is humble servant of this mystery, summoning humankind to nothing but the life-giving cross of Christ as the axis of a world made new. The rite for enrolling catechumens is clear and adamant about this.[26]

Second, the texts and rites of the whole reformed initiatory polity issued since the Second Vatican Council, together with their basic setting in the restored paschal season from the first Sunday of Lent through the Easter Vigil and on to Pentecost Sunday, must be factored into the process by which a theological nuancing of the conventionally Augustinian accents on original sin and the necessity of baptism takes place. Between the restored rites in their paschal setting on one hand, and the stresses on the need for *quamprimum* baptism of infants on the other, certain tensions exist that need resolution in a changed theological and pastoral climate.[27] This will have to be done with a certain theological elegance and within a hermeneutic based upon the maxim that the law of worship (the liturgical texts and rites, their setting, *and* the experience of their developing use) constitutes the law of belief (the doctrines of original sin and the necessity of baptism in their conventional Augustinian cast): *legem credendi lex statuat supplicandi*. Ancillary to this fundamental method, relatively recent research into the philosophy[28] and psychology[29] of human personality development can be brought to bear upon the dialectical process by which human growth and faith interact upon each other. If competently done, such a nuancing of the doctrines of original sin and the necessity of baptism should gradually move Catholic awareness away from a certain ritual obsession with *quamprimum* baptism that has tended to dismember the sacramental sequence of initiation, thus warping the intelligibility of its several phases and diminishing its pastoral effects in the Church. It should also, so far from rupturing the Roman

Church's continuity with its past, put the Church back in touch with some of the deepest wellsprings of its own tradition—sources which antedate medieval Christendom and are thus capable of being rich points for future development in a post-Christendom world.

Third, one of the most pregnant theological assertions in the document concerning the Christian initiation of adults is, as we have noted, that of [34], which relates confirmation to baptism in the strongest terms:

"This connection signifies the unity of the paschal mystery, the close relationship [*necessitudo*] between the mission of the Son and the pouring out of the Holy Spirit, and the joint celebration of the sacraments by which the Son and the Spirit come with the Father upon those who are baptized."

If the theology expressed here is taken seriously, then it is inevitable that the continued separation of baptism in infancy from confirmation must be reviewed. The alternative will be to sustain two different sets of meanings, catecheses, and ritual forms for the "sealing" of confirmation. The first will be that for adults and children of catechetical age who are baptized, confirmed, and communicated within the same liturgical event even if the bishop is absent. The second will be that for children and others who are baptized years previously. The sacramental ethos of the first is directly baptismal, paschal, and trinitarian: that of the second has more to do with marking an educational or life-crisis point in the personal development of the recipients, and it is enhanced by the presence of the bishop at the event.

The Roman Rite thus finds itself affirming in practice *two* initiatory theories and polities that have successively held sway in its history: the first is antique and paschal, meant to consecrate and initiate a Christian wholly; the second is medieval and socio-personal in emphasis, stressing "growth" on all fronts (*ad robur*). The first presupposes the presence of catechumens in local churches together with the evangelical and catechetical structures necessary to prepare them for baptism. The second presupposes a sustained Catholic birthrate and functioning forms of religious education such as the parochial school. The two project rather different models of the Church as well, the second being a "Christendom model" currently wracked with enervating problems that arise not from the hostility of the modern state so much as from its massive indifference. The first projected model, on the contrary, does not presuppose the state at all: it was, in fact, developed historically not only without recourse to state benevolence but often in opposition to its pretensions. That there is a growing awareness of a drift of history away from the second model and toward the first is perhaps signaled by recent addresses to the Church on the matter of *evangelization* from no less than Pope Paul VI, the world Synod of Bishops, and the American Catholic hierarchy.

Be this as it may, the juxtaposition of two distinct sets of initiatory theories and practices cannot but affect them both. One might suggest that while the juxtaposition reflects the reality of the Church's position at present and perhaps for some time to come, the more paschal and antique polity will, granted the fact of our being a Church in a post-Christendom world, eventually prevail in some form. If one is correct in this assessment it means that the days of baptism in infancy and confirmation years later as the norm are numbered. That the days of evangelization through social structures sustained by a sympathetic state are numbered. That the days of catechizing solely in classrooms according to strictly "educational" techniques are numbered. That the days in which a man's or woman's entry into a novitiate or seminary could be spoken of as their "entry into the Church" are numbered. That the days of a practical correlation between Church and civil society are over. It should be possible to test the validity of these propositions by the degree to which the initiatory polity of the *Rite of Christian Initiation of Adults* is found to be irresistible in practice. Theological reflection upon sacramental meaning and the nature of the Church will have to keep pace with the growth of the practice. The latter could well stimulate the creation of a true and contemporary *pastoral* theology that sinks its roots deep into the lived experience of the Church rather than into books issuing from academe.

Fourth, and finally, the creation of such a true *pastoral* theology will quickly discover that its central concern has to do with reflecting anew on conversion as the genesis of the Church. Most particularly this reflection will emphasize the ecclesial rather than the purely individualistic dimensions and effects of conversion. For in Catholic tradition at its best, faith is not a creedal confession that gives rise to certain forms of life: faith is, rather, a definite way of life in common that generates creedal confessions not as surrogates for but as symptoms of its vitality. In this sense, the Church is neither a religion nor a denomination. It is simply the way a re-created world coheres in constant praise and adoration of him who is its source. Any theology of conversion that cannot bear this cosmological weight will never produce a grasp of evangelization, catechesis, or sacramental initiation rich enough to support the life of communion in faith the gospel of Jesus Christ gives rise to and the Church Catholic presumes in its members. It is a life to which, literally, nothing human is foreign save sin: a life so incarnationally septic as to be thus altogether glorious.

SUMMARY

This book has attempted to analyze the Roman initiatory tradition and to interpret its new *Rite of Christian Initiation of Adults* in an effort to show why and how the latter serves as a primary means of expressing and causing Christian identity both individual and communal. It began with the New Testament's insistence on the necessity of baptism in Christ as new birth and as consummation of the themes of cleansing, passage, and solidarity found in Israel. The exodus and passion narratives recount in phase both Israel's and the Son of Man's passage from slavery and limit to filiation and freedom. Christian initiation traverses the same passage from "shame" to "celebration," from the conviction of sin to the appropriation of sin's complete forgiveness in Christ. The ritualization of baptismal structures provided the central occasion in Church life whereby Christ's own passage from death to life and cleansing from "sin" could be appropriated ever anew, a regular paschal experience that kept firm the paradigm by which the Church was to carry out its mission, govern its existence, and be judged by God.

In this cleansing passage through the rites of baptism in its fullness ordinary conventions, social patterns, and ways of perception are suspended, altered, reversed, and transcended. As a result of this process, the complex of baptismal rites (from entry into the catechumenate and before, through the water bath and anointing with Spirit, to the eucharist and beyond) become "anti-structural" in character.[30] Anti-structure is primarily expressed in the phenomena of liminality (a sense of being in-between or on the threshold of two different states of existence) and *communitas* (a relatively unstructured, spontaneous, and undifferentiated communion of individuals). Baptism in its fullness is the primary liminal experience during which the Church is shaped each paschal season into a *communitas* of equals in one Body of neither Jew nor Greek, master nor slave, male nor female, and is prepared to receive fresh and new God's grace in Jesus the Anointed One now become life-giving Spirit. In its catechumens, the Church passes in him from death to life each year at the *pascha*, being cleansed, reformed, renewed, and reintegrated. The anti-structural ethos of the Church's initiatory rites is in evidence throughout—in the "strangeness" of the time of the sacraments' celebration in the depths of night; in the radical egalitarianism of the candidates' near or total nakedness; in the numinous and elemental power of the taste of food, the smell of perfume, the feel of oil on the skin, the touch of others' hands, the sound of solemn words and ovations and singing, the sight of light shimmering and the sensation of being forced into deep water.

This interpretation of the *Rite of Christian Initiation of Adults* can come to no other conclusion than that it is normative for all other aspects of initiatory polity in the Roman Rite. This is due to the power of its contents, its vision of the Church baptizing, the scope of its view of conversion, and the post-Christendom pastoral context it implicitly both diagnoses and prognosticates. Its quality and its contemporaneity, furthermore, are in direct contact with the best of the Roman Rite's tradition on the matter of how a Christian is "made." It represents a demanding discipline of both catechumen and Church, but it never gives way to the temptations of an arrogant religious enthusiasm or of a rarified elitism of the saved. Its purpose is not to produce a passive proletariat whose rights must be carefully doled out piecemeal by an ordained aristocracy. Its purpose is to generate a People shot through with a style worthy of the gospel, with a finely disciplined humility before God's grace in Christ—a Spirited People irresistible in the splendid catholicity of its human and divine scope, unconquerable in the fulfillment of its mission in the world

Yet all this begins in the tortuous coils of each human being, touched by grace, coming to faith amid the commonwealth of that Spirit-filled Body of Christ which is the Church. These are those whom Tertullian addressed long ago in words fit to end this book as they ended his.

"Therefore, you blessed ones, for whom the grace of God is waiting, when you come up from that most sacred washing of the new birth, and when for the first time you spread out your hands with your brethren in your mother's house, ask of your Father, ask of your Lord, that special grants of grace and apportionments of spiritual gifts be yours. *Ask*, he says, *and ye shall receive*. So now, you have sought, and have found: you have knocked, and it has been opened to you. This only I pray, that as you ask you also have in mind Tertullian, a sinner."[31]

NOTES

1. See Charles Davis, *Sacraments of Initiation: Baptism and Confirmation* (Sheed and Ward, New York 1964) 113.

2. Thus G. Kretschmar, "Recent Research on Christian Initiation," *Studia Liturgica* 10:2/3 (1977) 89, in resumé of B. Neunheuser, *Baptism and Confirmation* (1964).

3. See the *Rite of Christian Initiation of Adults* 8.

4. Para. 14.

5. Para. 9.

6. Para. 15.

7. Helpful in this regard is John A. Berntsen, "Christian Affections and the Catechumenate," *Worship* 52 (1978) 194-210.

8. Para. 18 and 19:3.

9. Thus canon 87: *Baptismate homo constituitur in Ecclesia Christi persona cum omnibus christianorum iuribus et officiis, nisi, ad iura quod attinet, obstet obex, ecclesiasticae communionis vinculum impediens, vel lata ab Ecclesia censura.*

10. Thus the *Decree on the Ministry and Life of Priests* 5 (Abbott 542): "Hence the Eucharist shows itself to be the source and the apex of the whole work of preaching the gospel. Those under instruction are introduced by stages to a sharing in the Eucharist. The faithful, already marked with the sacred seal of baptism and confirmation, are through the reception of the Eucharist fully joined to the Body of Christ." In the final draft of this statement, "fully" (*plene*) replaced "more fully" (*plenius*), a change that marked a growth in theological maturity on the Council's part and a significant outstripping of conventional modes of thinking and speaking about baptism, confirmation, and eucharist. See also the *Pastoral Constitution on the Church in the Modern World* 38 (Abbott 235-237).

11. See Jonathan Z. Smith, "The Influence of Symbols upon Social Change: A Place on Which to Stand," *The Roots of Ritual*, ed. James D. Shaughnessy (Wm. B. Eerdmans Publishing Co., Grand Rapids, Michigan 1973) 121-143.

12. See Kent C. Bloomer and Charles W. Moore, *Body, Memory, and Architecture* (Yale University Press, New Haven 1977) 34-36 and 37-55. Also Mary Douglas, *Natural Symbols: Explorations in Cosmology* (Pantheon, New York 1970) passim.

13. See above, p. 130.

14. Note para. 7 and 296.

15. As the *Constitution on the Sacred Liturgy* 26 (Abbott 147) notes: "Liturgical services are not private functions, but are celebrations of the Church, which is the 'sacrament of unity,' namely, a holy people united and organized under their bishops. Therefore liturgical services pertain to the whole body of the Church; they manifest it and have effects on it . . . "

16. See pp. 169f.

17. See the *Constitution on the Sacred Liturgy* 28-32 (Abbott 148).

18. The two are distinct: see para. 42-43.

19. Thus para. 299.

20. Thus canon 732:1; the *General Introduction* to Christian Initiation, para 4.

21. Thus para. 297.

22. This seems implied in para. 295, although it is never stated in so many words.

23. Para. 304, emphasis added.

24. There follows the restriction of confirmation, quoted above, in the bishop's or extraordinary minister's absence.

25. *Extraordinarius minister est presbyter, cui vel iure communi vel peculiari Sedis Apostolicae indulto ea facultas concessa sit.*

26. Para. 75-97.

27. See above, pp. 89-91.

28. For some theological applications of philosophical personalism to sacramental baptism, see E. Schillebeeckx, *Christ the Sacrament of the Encounter with God* (Sheed and Ward, New York 1963) 109-112.

29. E.g., the research of Eric Erikson. For a resumé see Aidan Kavanagh, "The Role of Ritual in Personal Development," in *The Roots of Ritual* 145-160.

30. See Victor Turner, *The Ritual Process: Structure and Anti-Structure* (Aldine Publishing Company, Chicago 1969); "Passages, Margins, and Poverty: Religious Symbols of Communitas," *Worship* 46 (1972) 390-412, 482-494.

31. *On Baptism* 20 (Evans 43).

Bibliography

The following titles all appear in the notes. Comments on the book or article are sometimes added either in the notes or in this bibliography, which is divided into sections devoted to sources and to literature about the sources.

SOURCES

Ambrose. *On the Sacraments and On the Mysteries*, trans. T. Thompson, ed. J. H. Srawley. SPCK, London 1966.

Ambrose of Milan. *Concerning the Sacraments* and *Concerning the Mysteries*. In Whitaker, *Documents of the Baptismal Liturgy* (q.v.) 117-123.

Andrieu, Michel. *Les Ordines Romani du Haute Moyen Age*. Spicilegium Sacrum Lovaniense, Louvain 1931-1956. 4 vols.

The Apostolic Constitutions. In Whitaker, *Documents of the Baptismal Liturgy* 27-32.

Augustine: The First Catechetical Instruction, ed. J. P. Christopher. Regnery Logos Books, Chicago 1966.

The Awe-Inspiring Rites of Initiation: Baptismal Homilies of the Fourth Century, ed. Edward Yarnold. St. Paul Publications, Slough, England 1971. A collection of sources with some commentary.

The Babylonian Talmud, ed. I. Epstein. Soncino Press, London 1960-1974. 11 vols.

Baptism: Ancient Liturgies and Patristic Texts, ed. A. Hamman. Alba House, Staten Island 1967.

The Barberini Euchologion. In Whitaker, *Documents of the Baptismal Liturgy* 60-73.

The Bobbio Missal. In Whitaker, *Documents of the Baptismal Liturgy* 194-203.

Chavasse, A. *Le Sacramentaire Gélasien: Sacramentaire presbytéral en usage dans les titres romaines au VIIe siècle*. Bibliotheque de Théologie 4: Histoire de Théologie 1, Tournai 1958.

Clement of Rome. *The First Epistle of Clement to the Corinthians*. In *The Apostolic Fathers*, vol. I, ed. Kirsopp Lake, Loeb Classical Library series, 9-121. G. P. Putnam's Sons, New York 1919.

Codex Iuris Canonici. Typis Polyglottis Vaticanis, Vatican City 1918.

St. Cyril of Jerusalem's Lectures on the Christian Sacraments, ed. F. L. Cross. SPCK, London 1966.

Cyril of Jerusalem. *Mystagogical Catecheses*. In Whitaker, *Documents of the Baptismal Liturgy* 24-27.

The Didache, or Teaching of the Twelve Apostles. In *The Apostolic Fathers*, vol. I, ed. Kirsopp Lake, Loeb Classical Library series, 305-333. G. P. Putnam's Sons, New York 1919. Chapter 7 is also in Whitaker, *Documents of the Baptismal Liturgy* 1.

Didascalia Apostolorum. In Whitaker, *Documents of the Baptismal Liturgy* 9-10.

The Documents of Vatican II, ed. Walter M. Abbott. America Press, New York 1966.

Hedegård, D., ed. *Seder R. Amram Gaon*. Lindstedts Universitetsbokhandel, Lund 1951.

Hippolytus. *The Apostolic Tradition*. In Whitaker, *Documents of the Baptismal Liturgy* 2-7.

Ignatius of Antioch. *Letter to the Smyrnaeans*. In *The Apostolic Fathers*, vol. I, ed. Kirsopp Lake, Loeb Classical Library series, 251-267. G. P. Putnam's Sons, New York 1919.

Inscriptiones Latinae Christianae Veteres, ed. E. Diehl, vol. 1, 289. Weidmann, Berlin 1925.

St. John Chrysostom: Baptismal Instructions, ed. P. W. Harkins, Ancient Christian Writers series 31. Westminster Publishing Company, Westminster, Maryland 1963.

Liber Sacramentorum Romanae Aeclesiae Ordinis Anni Circuli [The Gelasian Sacramentary], ed. Cunibert Mohlberg. Herder, Rome 1968.

The Mishnah, ed. H. Danby. The Clarendon Press, Oxford 1949.

Ordo Initiationis Christianae Adultorum. Typis Polyglottis Vaticanis, Vatican City 1972.

Rite of Baptism for Children. United States Catholic Conference, Washington, D.C. 1969.

Rite of Christian Initiaton of Adults. United States Catholic Conference, Washington, D.C. 1974.

Rite of Confirmation. National Conference of Catholic Bishops; Bishops' Committee on the Liturgy, Washington, D.C. 1974.

The Rites of the Catholic Church. Pueblo Publishing Company, New York 1976. This volume contains all the new Roman rites except the eucharist, the liturgy of the hours, and the major ordinations. Subsequent editions of it will keep the rites it contains up to date with any subsequent modifications made in them by ecclesiastical authority.

The Stowe Missal. In Whitaker, *Documents of the Baptismal Liturgy* 203-211.

Tertullian. *De Corona*. In Whitaker, *Documents of the Baptismal Liturgy* 9.

———. *On Baptism*. In *Tertullian's Homily on Baptism*, ed. Ernest Evans. SPCK, London 1964. Certain chapters are excerpted in Whitaker, *Documents of the Baptismal Liturgy* 7-9.

Thomas, The Acts of Judas. In Whitaker, *Documents of the Baptismal Liturgy* 10-16.

Whitaker, E. C., ed. *Documents of the Baptismal Liturgy*. SPCK, London 1960. An indispensable resource in English of baptismal texts from the early centuries.

LITERATURE

Adult Baptism and the Catechumenate, ed. Johannes Wagner, Concilium Series 22. Paulist Press, New York 1967.

Aland, Kurt. *Did the Early Church Baptize Infants?* trans. G. R. Beasley-Murray. Westminster Press, Philadelphia 1963.

Aubry, André. "Le projet pastoral du rituel de l'initiation des adultes." *Ephemerides Liturgicae* 88 (1974) 174-191.

Audet, J.-P. *La didache. Instruction des Apôtres*. Librarie Lecoffre, Paris 1958.

Andrieu, Michel. "L'ordo XI et les sacramentaires romaines." In *Les Ordines Romani du Haute Moyen Age*, vol. 2, 380-408. Spicilegium Sacrum Lovaniense, Louvain 1948.

Baptism in the New Testament. A Symposium, trans. D. Askew. Geoffrey Chapman, London 1964.

Barth, Karl. *The Teaching of the Church Regarding Baptism*, trans. E. A. Payne. SCM Press, London 1948.

Barth, Markus. *Die Taufe: ein Sakrament?* Evangelischer Verlag, Zollikon-Zurich 1951.

Baumstark, Anton. *Comparative Liturgy*, trans. F. L. Cross. A. R. Mowbray, London [3]1958.

Beasley-Murray, G. R. *Baptism in the New Testament*. Macmillan, New York 1962.

Béraudy, Roger. "Scrutinies and Exorcisms." In *Adult Baptism and the Catechumenate*, ed. Johannes Wagner, Concilium Series 22, 57-61. Paulist Press, New York 1967.

Berntsen, John A. "Christian Affections and the Catechumenate." *Worship* 52 (1978) 194-210.

Bloomer, Kent C., and Charles W. Moore. *Body, Memory, and Architecture*. Yale University Press, New Haven 1977.

Bouyer, L. *The Decomposition of Catholicism*, trans. C. U. Quinn. Franciscan Herald Press, Chicago 1969.

Brinkhoff, L. "Chronicle of the Liturgical Movement." In *Liturgy in Development*, ed. Alting von Geusau, 40-67. Sheed and Ward Stagbooks, London 1965.

Brock, Sebastian. "Studies in the Early History of the Syrian Orthodox Baptismal Liturgy." *Journal of Theological Studies* 23 (1972) 16-64.

———."The Syrian Baptismal Ordines," *Studia Liturgica* 12:4 (1978) 177-183.

Brown, Peter. *The World of Late Antiquity*. Thames and Hudson, London 1971.

Brunner, Emil. *Truth as Encounter*. Westminster Press, Philadelphia 1964.

———. *Wahrheit als Begegnung*. Zwingli-Verlag, Zurich 1938.

Bugnini, A. *Documenta Pontificia ad Instaurationem Liturgicam*. Editione Liturgiche, Rome 1953.

Camelot, P.-T. "La théologie de la Confirmation à la lumière des controverses recentes." *La Maison-Dieu* 54 (1958) 79-91.

———. "Sur la théologie de la confirmation." *Revue des Sciences Philosophiques et Théologiques* 38 (1954) 637-657.

———. "Toward a Theology of Confirmation." *Theology Digest* 7 (1959) 67-71.

Carré, A. M. *Baptized in Christ*, trans. S. W. Giffiths. The Liturgical Press, Collegeville, Minnesota 1957.

Christiaens, J. "L'organisation d'un catéchuménat au XVIe siècle." *La Maison-Dieu* 58 (1959) 71-82.

Cote, Wolfred Nelson. *The Archaeology of Baptism*. Yates and Alexander, London 1876.

Cullmann, Oscar. *Baptism in the New Testament*, trans. J. K. S. Reid. SCM Press, London 1950.

Dahl, Nils. "The Origin of Baptism." In *Interpretationes ad Vetus Testamentum pertinentes Sigmundo Mowinckel*, 36-52. Forlaget Land og Kirke, Oslo 1955.

Dalmais, I. H. "La Liturgie et la dépôt de la foi." In *L'Eglise en Prière*, ed. A. G. Martimort *et al.*, 220-228. Desclée, Paris 1961.

Daniélou, J. *The Bible and the Liturgy*. University of Notre Dame Press, Notre Dame, Indiana 1956.

Davis, Charles. *Sacraments of Initiation: Baptism and Confirmation*. Sheed and Ward, New York 1964. Published in England as *The Making of a Christian*.

Delorme, J. "The Practice of Baptism in Judaism at the Beginning of the Christian Era." In *Baptism in the New Testament. A Symposium*, trans. D. Askew, 25-60. Geoffrey Chapman, London 1964.

Dix, Gregory. *The Shape of the Liturgy*. Dacre Press, London 1945.

———. *The Theology of Confirmation in Relation to Baptism*. Dacre Press, London 1946.

Douglas, Mary. *Natural Symbols. Explorations in Cosmology*. Pantheon, New York 1970.

———. *Purity and Danger. An Analysis of Concepts of Pollution and Taboo*. Routledge and Kegan Paul, London 1966.

Dujarier, Michel. "Sponsorship." In *Adult Baptism and the Catechumenate*, ed. Johannes Wagner, Concilium Series 22, 45-50. Paulist Press, New York 1967.

Fischer, Balthasar. "Baptismal Exorcism in the Catholic Baptismal Rites after Vatican II." *Studia Liturgica* 10:1 (1974) 48-55.

Fisher, J. D. C. *Christian Initiation. Baptism in the Medieval West*. SPCK, London 1965.

———. *Christian Initiation. The Reformation Period*. SPCK, London 1970.

Flemington, W. F. *The New Testament Doctrine of Baptism*. SPCK, London 1957.

Fuller, Reginald. "Christian Initiation in the New Testament." In *Made, Not Born*, 7-31. University of Notre Dame Press, Notre Dame, Indiana 1976.

Grant, Robert. "Development of the Christian Catechumenate." In *Made, Not Born*, 32-49. University of Notre Dame Press, Notre Dame, Indiana 1976.

Gy, P.-M. "The Idea of 'Christian Initiation.'" *Studia Liturgica* 12:2/3 (1977) 172-175.

Hanssens, J. M. *La Liturgie d'Hippolyte*. Oriental Institute, Rome 1959.

Heris, Ch.-V. "Le salut des enfants morts sans baptême." *La Maison-Dieu* 10 (1947) 86-105.

Hovda, Robert. "Hope for the Future: A Summary." In *Made, Not Born*, 152-167. University of Notre Dame Press, Notre Dame, Indiana 1976.

James, E. O. *Christian Myth and Ritual. A Historical Study*. J. Murray, London 1933.

Jeremias, Joachim. *Die Kindertaufe in den ersten vier Jahrhunderten*. Vandenhoeck & Ruprecht, Göttingen 1958.

———. *Infant Baptism in the First Four Centuries*, trans. D. Cairns. Westminster Press, Philadelphia 1962.

Jungmann, J. A. *The Mass of the Roman Rite*, trans. F. X. Brunner, 2 vols. Benziger, New York 1950.

———. *The Place of Christ in Liturgical Prayer*, trans. A. Peeler. Alba House, Staten Island [2]1965.

Kavanagh, Aidan. "Initiation: Baptism and Confirmation." *Worship* 46 (1972) 262-276.

———. "Teaching Through the Liturgy." *Notre Dame Journal of Education* 5:1 (1974) 35-47.

———. "The Role of Ritual in Personal Development." In *The Roots of Ritual*, ed. James D. Shaughnessy, 145-160. Wm. B. Eerdmans Publishing Company, Grand Rapids, Michigan 1973.

———."What is Participation?" *Doctrine and Life* 23 (1973) 343-353.

Keifer, Ralph. "Christian Initiation: The State of the Question." In *Made, Not Born*, 138-151. University of Notre Dame Press, Notre Dame, Indiana 1976.

Kelly, J. N. D. *Early Christian Creeds*. Longmans, Green, London 1950.

Kretschmar, Georg. "Die Geschichte des Taufgottesdienstes in der alten Kirche." In *Leitourgia. Handbuch des evangelischen Gottesdienstes* 5, 1-348. J. Stauda Verlag, Kassel 1970.

———. "Recent Research on Christian Initiation." *Studia Liturgica* 12:2/3 (1977) 87-103.

Lampe, G. W. H. "Baptism and Confirmation in the Light of the Fathers." In *Becoming a Christian*, ed. B. Minchin. Faith Press, London 1954.

———. *The Seal of the Spirit. A Study in the Doctrine of Baptism and Confirmation in the New Testament and the Fathers.* SPCK, London [2]1967.

Leenhardt, F.-J. *Le Baptême chrétien, son origine, sa signification*. Delachaux & Niestlé, Neuchâtel 1946.

L'Eglise en Prière, ed. A. G. Martimort *et al.* Desclée, Paris 1961. A helpful manual of liturgical studies, part of which has been translated into English as *The Church at Prayer*, trans. R. Fisher *et al.* Irish University Press, New York 1968.

Lukken, G. M. *Original Sin in the Roman Liturgy. Research into the Theology of Original Sin in the Roman Sacramentaria and the Early Baptismal Liturgy*. E. J. Brill, Leiden 1973.

Made, Not Born. New Perspectives on Christian Initiation and the Catechumenate, ed. Murphy Center for Liturgical Research. University of Notre Dame Press, Notre Dame, Indiana 1976.

Maertens, Thierry. *Histoire et pastorale du rituel du catéchuménat et du Baptême*. Publications de Saint-André, Bruges 1962.

Marcel, P. C. *The Biblical Doctrine of Infant Baptism: Sacrament of the Covenant of Grace*, trans. P. E. Hughes. J. Clarke & Co., London 1953.

Martimort, A. G. *The Signs of the New Covenant*. The Liturgical Press, Collegeville, Minnesota 1963.

Marx, Paul B. *Virgil Michel and the Liturgical Movement*. The Liturgical Press, Collegeville, Minnesota 1957.

Mason, A. J. *The Relation of Confirmation to Baptism*. Longmans, Green, London 1891.

Meagher, John. *The Gathering of the Ungifted*. Seabury, New York 1973.

Michel, Virgil. "Confirmation: Call to Battle." *Orate Fratres* 2 (1928) 234-239.

———."Confirmation: Its Divine Powers." *Orate Fratres* 2 (1928) 199-204.

———. "Confirmation: Our Apathy." *Orate Fratres* 2 (1928) 167-171.

Mitchell, Leonel L. "Christian Initiation: The Reformation Period." In *Made, Not Born*, 83-98. University of Notre Dame Press, Notre Dame, Indiana 1976.

Mitchell, Nathan. "Dissolution of the Rite of Christian Initiation." In *Made, Not Born*, 50-82. University of Notre Dame Press, Notre Dame, Indiana 1976.

Moody, Dale. *Baptism: Foundation for Christian Unity*. Westminster Press, Philadelphia 1967.

Moreton, Bernard. *The Eighth-Century Gelasian Sacramentary*. Oxford University Press, Oxford 1976.

Neunheuser, B. *Baptism and Confirmation*, trans. John Jay Hughes. Herder and Herder, New York 1964.

Potel, J. *Moins de baptêmes en France. Pourquoi?* Les Editions du Cerf, Paris 1974.

Rahner, K. *The Church and the Sacraments*, trans. W. J. O'Hara. Herder and Herder, New York 1963.

Ramsey, Paul. "Protecting the Unborn." *Commonweal* 100 (31 May 1974) 308-314.

Reinhold, Hans Ansgar. *The American Parish and the Roman Liturgy*. Macmillan, New York 1958.

———. *H. A. R. The Autobiography of Father Reinhold*, with foreword by W. H. Auden. Herder and Herder, New York 1968.

Rieff, Philip. *The Triumph of the Therapeutic: Uses of Faith after Freud*. Harper and Row, New York 1966.

Riley, Hugh M. *Christian Initiation: A Comparative Study of the Interpretation of the Baptismal Liturgy in the Mystagogical Writings of Cyril of Jerusalem, John Chrysostom, Theodore of Mopsuestia, and Ambrose of Milan*. Catholic University of America Press, Washington, D. C. 1974.

Robeyns, Anselme. "Rights of the Baptized." *Theology Digest* 10 (1962) 106-112.

Roguet, A. M. *Christ Acts Through the Sacraments*, trans. by the Carisbrooke Dominicans. The Liturgical Press, Collegeville, Minnesota 1954.

Rowell, G. *The Liturgy of Christian Burial. An Introductory Survey of the Historical Development of Christian Burial Rites*. SPCK, London 1977.

Schmemann, Alexander. *Of Water and the Spirit.* St. Vladimir's Seminary Press, New York 1974.

———. "Theology and Liturgical Tradition." In *Worship in Scripture and Tradition*, ed. Massey H. Shepherd, 165-178. Oxford University Press, Oxford 1963.

Schillebeeckx, E. *Christ the Sacrament of the Encounter with God*. Sheed and Ward, New York 1963.

Schmidt, H. *Hebdomada Sancta*. Herder, Rome 1957.

Schnackenburg, R. *Baptism in the Thought of St. Paul*, trans. G. R. Beasley-Murray. Blackwell, Oxford 1964.

Smith, Jonathan Z. "The Influence of Symbols upon Social Change: A Place on Which to Stand." In *The Roots of Ritual*, ed. James D. Shaughnessy, 121-143. Wm. B. Eerdmans Publishing Co., Grand Rapids, Michigan 1973.

Stenzel, Alois. *Die Taufe: eine genetische Erklärung der Taufliturgie*. Verlag Felizian Rauch, Innsbruck 1958. One of the best compact historical treatments of baptism, unfortunately not yet translated into English.

———. "Temporal and Supra-Temporal in the History of the Catechumenate and Baptism." In *Adult Baptism and the Catechumenate*, ed. Johannes Wagner, Concilium Series 22, 31-44. Paulist Press, New York 1967.

Thornton, L. S. *Confirmation: Its Place in the Baptismal Mystery*. Dacre Press, London 1954.

Thurian, Max. *La confirmation. Consécration des laïcs*. Delachaux & Niestlé, Neuchâtel 1957.

Turner, Victor. "Passages, Margins, and Poverty: Religious Symbols of Communitas." *Worship* 46 (1972) 390-412 and 482-494.

———. *The Ritual Process: Structure and Anti-Structure*. Aldine Publishing Company, Chicago 1969.

van der Meer, F. *Augustine the Bishop*, trans. B. Battershaw and G. R. Lamb. Sheed and Ward, New York 1961.

Wainwright, G. "The Rites and Ceremonies of Christian Initiation." *Studia Liturgica* 10:1 (1974) 2-24.

Winkler, Gabriele. *Das armenische Initiationsrituale. Entwicklungsgeschichtliche und liturgievergleichende Untersuchung der Quellen des 3. bis 10. Jahrhunderts*. Oriental Institute, Rome 1979.

———. "The Original Meaning of the Prebaptismal Anointing and Its Implications." *Worship* 52 (1978) 24-45.

Worship in Scripture and Tradition, ed. Massey H. Shepherd. Oxford University Press, Oxford 1963.

Index